A DOLL'S HOUSE

Henrik Ibsen

AUTHORED by Robert William
UPDATED AND REVISED by Adam Kissel

COVER DESIGN by Table XI Partners LLC
COVER PHOTO by Olivia Verma and © 2005 GradeSaver, LLC

BOOK DESIGN by Table XI Partners LLC

Published by GradeSaver LLC, www.gradesaver.com

First published in the United States of America by GradeSaver LLC. 2008

ISBN 978-1-60259-144-8

Printed in the United States of America

Table of Contents

Table of Contents

Biography of Henrik Ibsen (1828-1906)

Henrik Johan Ibsen, born in 1828 in Skien, Norway, was the eldest of five children after the early death of his older brother. His father, Knud Ibsen, one in a long line of sea captains, had been born in Skien in 1797 and had married Marichen Cornelia Martie Altenburg, the daughter of a German merchant, in 1825. Though Ibsen later reported that Skien was a pleasant place to grow up, his childhood was not particularly happy. He was described as an unsociable child. His sense of isolation increased at the age of sixteen when his father's business had to be sold to meet the demands of his creditors. On top of this, a rumor began circulating that Henrik was the illegitimate son of another man. Although the rumor was never proven to be true, it manifested itself in the theme of illegitimate offspring that runs throughout Ibsen's later works.

After Knud's business was repossessed, all that remained of the family's former estate was a dilapidated farmhouse on the outskirts of Skein. It was there that Ibsen began to attend the small, middle-class school where he cultivated a talent for painting, if nothing else. He was also taught German and Latin as well as drawing. In 1843, at the age of fifteen, Ibsen was confirmed and taken from the school. Though he had declared his interest in becoming a painter, Ibsen was apprenticed to an apothecary shortly before his sixteenth birthday.

Leaving his family, Ibsen traveled to Grimstad, a small, isolated town, to begin his apprenticeship. He maintained a strong desire to gain admission to the university to study medicine. Meanwhile, he fathered an illegitimate son with the maid of the apothecary. Despite his unhappy lot, Ibsen began to write in earnest in Grimstad. Inspired by the European revolutions of 1848, Ibsen wrote satire and elegant poetry.

At the age of twenty-one, Ibsen left Grimstad for the capital. While in Christiania (now Oslo), Ibsen passed his exams but opted not to pursue his education, instead turning to playwriting and journalism. In Christiania he penned his first play, *Catiline* (1849), written in blank verse about the failure of Catiline's conspiracy against ancient Rome in the time of Cicero. It sold only 45 copies and was rejected by every theater Ibsen submitted it to for performance. Ibsen also spent time analyzing and criticizing modern Norwegian literature.

Still poor, Ibsen gladly accepted a contract to write for and help manage the newly constituted National Theater in Bergen in 1851. Beginning his work untrained and largely uneducated, Ibsen soon learned much from his time at the theater, producing such works as *St. John's Night* (1852). The majority of his writings from this period were based on folksongs, folklore, and history.

In 1858, Ibsen moved back to Christiania to become the creative director of the city's Norwegian Theater. That same year, Ibsen married Suzannah Thoresen, with whom he fathered a child named Sigurd Ibsen. Though his plays suggest otherwise, Ibsen revered the state of marriage, believing that it was possible for two people to travel through life as perfect, happy equals. During this period, Ibsen also developed a daily routine from which he would not deviate until his first stroke in 1901: he would rise, consume a small breakfast, take a long walk, write for five hours, eat dinner, and finish the night with entertainment or early retirement to bed.

Despite this routine, Ibsen found his life difficult, though he did pen several plays, including *Love's Comedy* (1862), a close relation of *A Doll's House* (1879) in its distinction between love and marriage. Luckily, in 1864, his friends generously offered him money that they had collected, allowing him to move to Italy. He felt like an exile. He would spend the next twenty-seven years living in Italy and Germany. During this time abroad, he authored a number of successful works, including *Brand* (1866) and *Peer Gynt* (1867), both (significantly) written to be read rather than to be performed.

Ibsen moved to Dresden in 1868 and then to Munich in 1875. In Munich in 1879, Ibsen wrote his groundbreaking play, *A Doll's House*. He pursued his interest in realistic drama for the next decade, earning international acclaim; many of his works were published in translation and performed throughout Europe.

Ibsen eventually turned to a new style of writing, abandoning his interest in realism for a series of so-called symbolic dramas. He completed his last work, *Hedda Gabler*, abroad in 1890.

After being away from Norway for twenty-seven years, Ibsen and Suzannah returned in 1891. Shortly afterwards, he finished writing *The Master Builder* (1892), after which he took a short break. In late 1893, seemingly in need of moist air to help cure her recurring gout, Suzannah left for southern Italy. While his wife was away, Ibsen found a companion in a young female pianist, Hildur Andersen, with whom he spent a great deal of time. He continued to correspond with her even after Suzannah's return. Ibsen's relationship with Andersen was characteristic of his larger interest in the younger generation; he was famous for seeking out their ideas and encouraging their writing.

Ibsen's later plays tended to meet with controversy on the occasions of their first performances: *Hedda Gabler* was reviled by critics of the published script and of the first production in 1890. It is at about this time that Ibsen's work, partly as a consequence of George Bernard Shaw's lecture *The Quintessence of Ibsenism* (1890), became extremely popular in England.

After suffering a series of strokes, Ibsen died in 1906 at the age of seventy-eight. He was unable to write for the last five years of his life, following a stroke which also left him unable to walk. Reportedly his last words, after his nurse suggested he was doing better, were, "To the contrary!"

About A Doll's House

Ibsen's A Doll's House (1879), written while Ibsen was in Rome and Amalfi, Italy, was conceived at a time of revolution in Europe. Charged with the fever of the 1848 European revolutions, a new modern perspective was emerging in the literary and dramatic world, challenging the romantic tradition. It is Ibsen who can be credited for mastering and popularizing the realist drama derived from this new perspective. His plays were read and performed throughout Europe in numerous translations like almost no dramatist before. A Doll's House was published in Copenhagen, Denmark, where it premiered.

His success was particularly important for Norway and the Norwegian language. Having been freed from four centuries of Danish rule in 1814, Norway was just beginning to shake off the legacy of Danish domination. A Doll's House was written in a form of Norwegian that still bore heavy traces of Danish. Ibsen deliberately chose a colloquial language style to emphasize local realism, though Torvald Helmer does speak in what Michael Meyer has described as "stuffy Victorianisms." Ibsen quickly became Norway's most popular dramatic figure. But it is the universality of Ibsen's writings, particularly of A Doll's House, that has made this play an oft-performed classic (see "A Stage History" for details of the play in performance).

It is believed that the plot of A Doll's House was based on an event in Ibsen's own life. In 1870 Laura Kieler had sent Ibsen a sequel to *Brand*, called *Brand's Daughters*, and Ibsen had taken an interest in the pretty, vivacious girl, nicknaming her "the lark." He invited her to his home, and for two months in the summer of 1872, she visited his home constantly. When she married, a couple of years later, her husband fell ill and was advised to take a vacation in a warm climate–and Laura, like Nora does in the play, secretly borrowed money to finance the trip (which took place in 1876). Laura falsified a note, the bank refused payment, and she told her husband the whole story. He demanded a separation, removed the children from her care, and only took her back after she had spent a month in a public asylum.

Laura and Nora have similar-sounding names, but their stories diverge. In Ibsen's play, Nora never returns home, nor does she ever break the news to her husband. Moreover—here the difference is most striking—it is Nora who divorces her husband. The final act of the play reveals Torvald as generous and even sympathetic.

A Doll's House was the second in a series of realist plays by Ibsen. The first, *The Pillars of Society* (1877), had caused a stir throughout Europe, quickly spreading to the avant garde theaters of the island and the continent. In adopting the realist form, Ibsen abandoned his earlier style of saga plays, historical epics, and verse allegories. Ibsen's letters reveal that much of what is contained in his realist dramas is based on events from his own life. Indeed, he was particularly interested in the possibility of true wedlock as well as in women in general. He later would write a series of psychological studies focusing on women.

One of the most striking and oft-noted characteristics of A Doll's House is the way it challenges the technical tradition of the so-called well-made play in which the first act offers an exposition, the second a situation, and the third an unraveling. This was the standard form from the earliest fables until the time of A Doll's House, which helped usher in a new, alternative standard. Ibsen's play was notable for exchanging the last act's unraveling for a discussion, one which leaves the audience uncertain about how the events will conclude. Critics agree that, until the last moments of the play, A Doll's House could easily be just another modern drama broadcasting another comfortable moral lesson. Finally, however, when Nora tells Torvald that they must sit down and "discuss all this that has been happening between us," the play diverges from the traditional form. With this new technical feature, A Doll's House became an international sensation and founded a new school of dramatic art.

Additionally, A Doll's House subverted another dramatic tradition. Ibsen's realist drama disregarded the tradition of featuring an older male moral figure. Dr. Rank, the character who should serve this role, is far from a positive moral force. Instead, he is not only sickly, rotting from a disease picked up from his father's earlier sexual exploits, but also lascivious, openly coveting Nora. The choice to portray both Dr. Rank and the potentially matronly Mrs. Linde as imperfect humans seemed like a novel approach at the time.

The real complexity (as opposed to a stylized dramatic romanticism) of Ibsen's characters remains something of a challenge for actors. Many actresses find it difficult to portray both a silly, immature Nora in the first act or so and the serious, open-minded Nora of the end of the last act. Similarly, actors are challenged to portray the full depth of Torvald's character. Many are tempted to play him as a slimy, patronizing brute, disregarding the character's genuine range of emotion and conviction. Such complexity associates A Doll's House with the best of Western drama. The printed version of A Doll's House sold out even before it hit the stage.

A more obvious importance of A Doll's House is the feminist message that rocked the stages of Europe when the play premiered. Nora's rejection of marriage and motherhood scandalized contemporary audiences. In fact, the first German productions of the play in the 1880s used an altered ending, written by Ibsen at the request of the producers. Ibsen referred to this version as a "barbaric outrage" to be used only in emergencies.

The revolutionary spirit and the emergence of modernism influenced Ibsen's choice to focus on an unlikely hero, a housewife, in his attack on middle-class values. Quickly becoming the talk of parlors across Europe, the play succeeded in its attempt to provoke discussion. In fact, it is the numerous ways that the play can be read and interpreted that make the play so interesting. Each new generation has had a different way of interpreting the book, from seeing it as feminist critique to taking it as a Hegelian allegory of the spirit's historical evolution. This richness is another sign of its greatness.

Yet precisely what sort of play is it? George Steiner claims that the play is "founded on the belief…that women can and must be raised to the dignity of man," but Ibsen himself believed it to be more about the importance of self-liberation than the importance of specifically female liberation—yet his contemporary Strindberg certainly disagreed, himself calling the play a "barbaric outrage" because of the feminism he perceived it as promoting.

There are many comic sections in the play—one might argue that Nora's "songbird" and "squirrel" acts, as well as her early flirtatious conversations with her husband, are especially humorous. Still, like many modern productions, A Doll's House seems to fit the classical definition of neither comedy nor tragedy. Unusually for a traditional comedy, at the end there is a divorce, not a marriage, and the play implies that Dr. Rank could be dead as the final curtain falls. But this is not a traditional tragedy either, for the ending of A Doll's House has no solid conclusion. The ending notably is left wide open: there is no brutal event, no catharsis, just ambiguity. This is a play that defies boundaries.

Character List

Nora

The play's protagonist and the wife of Torvald Helmer, Nora has never lived alone, going immediately from the care of her father to that of her husband. Inexperienced in the ways of the world as a result of this sheltering, Nora is impulsive and materialistic. But the play questions the extent to which these attributes are mere masks that Nora uses to negotiate the patriarchal oppression she faces every day. The audience learns in the first act that Nora is independent enough to negotiate the loan to make Krogstad's holiday possible, and over the course of the play, Nora emerges as a fully independent woman who rejects both the false union of her marriage and the burden of motherhood.

Torvald

Nora's husband of eight years, Torvald Helmer, at the beginning of the play, has been promoted to manager of the bank. Torvald has built his middle-class living through his own work and not from family money. Focused on business, Torvald spends a great deal of his time at home in his study, avoiding general visitors and interacting very little with his children. In fact, he sees himself primarily as responsible for the financial welfare of his family and as a guardian for his wife. Torvald is particularly concerned with morality. He also can come across as stiff and unsympathetic. Still, the last act of the play makes very clear that he dearly loves his wife.

Dr. Rank

Friend of the family and Torvald's physician, Dr. Rank embodies and subverts the theatrical role of the male moral force that had been traditional in the plays of the time. Rather than providing moral guidance and example for the rest of the characters, Dr. Rank is a corrupting force, both physically and morally. Sick from consumption of the spine as a result of his father's sexual exploits, the Doctor confesses his desire for Nora in the second act and goes off to die in the third act, leaving a visiting card with a black cross to signify that--for him--the end has come.

Mrs. Linde

Sometimes given as Mrs. Linden (for example, in the 1890 translation by Henrietta Frances Lord). An old schoolmate of Nora's, Mrs. Christine Linde comes back into Nora's life after losing her husband and mother. She worked hard to support her helpless mother and two younger brothers since the death of her husband. Now, with her mother dead and her brothers being adults, she is a free agent. Pressed for money, Mrs. Linde successfully asks Nora to help her secure a job at Torvald's bank. Ultimately, Mrs. Linde decides that she will only be happy if she goes off with Krogstad. Her older, weary viewpoint provides a foil to Nora's youthful impetuousness. She perhaps also symbolizes a hollowness in the matriarchal role. Her relationship with Krogstad also provides a point of comparison with that of Nora and Torvald.

Krogstad

Nils Krogstad is a man from whom Nora borrows money to pay for trip to Italy, an acquaintance of Torvald's and an employee at the bank which Torvald has just taken over. Krogstad was involved in a work scandal many years previously; as a result, his name has been sullied and his career stunted. When his job at the bank is jeopardized by Torvald's refusal to work with a man he sees as hopelessly corrupt, Krogstad blackmails Nora to ensure that he does not lose his job.

Ivar, Bob, and Emmy

Nora's young children. Raised primarily by Anne, the Nurse (and Nora's old nurse), the children spend little time with their mother or father. The time they do spend with Nora consists of Nora playing with them as if she were just another playmate. The children speak no individualized lines; they are "Three Children." Ibsen facilitates their dialogue through Nora's mouth, and they are often cut entirely in performance.

Anne

The family nurse. Anne raised Nora, who had lost her mother, and stayed on to raise Nora's children. Nora is confident that she can leave her children in Anne's care.

Helen

A housemaid employed by the Helmers.

Porter

A porter who brings in the Christmas Tree at the very beginning.

Major Themes

Doll's House

The whole play takes place in one room. Until the last act, Nora is in every scene; she never seems to leave the room. The action of the play all comes to her. She is literally trapped in domestic comfort. She is given her "housekeeping" money by Helmer as though she is a doll in a doll's house. The play suggests that this treatment is condescending and not an appropriate way to treat one's wife.

Gender

This play focuses on the ways that women are perceived in their various roles, especially in marriage and motherhood. Torvald, in particular, has a very clear but narrow definition of women's roles. He believes that it is the sacred duty of a woman to be a good wife and mother. Moreover, he tells Nora that women are responsible for the morality of their children. In essence, he sees women as childlike, helpless creatures detached from reality on the one hand, but on the other hand as influential moral forces responsible for the purity of the world through their influence in the home.

Ideas of 'manliness' are present in more subtle ways. Nora's description of Torvald suggests that she is partially aware of the inconsistent pressures on male roles as much as the inconsistent pressures on female roles in their society. Torvald's own conception of manliness is based on the value of total independence. He abhors the idea of financial or moral dependence on anyone. His strong desire for independence may put him out of touch with the reality of human interdependence.

Frequent references to Nora's father often equate her with him because of her actions and her disposition. Although people think he gave Nora and Torvald the money for their trip to Italy, it was actually Nora. She has more agency and decision-making skills than she is given credit for. Nora seems to wish to enjoy the privileges and power enjoyed by males in her society. She seems to understand the confinement she faces simply by virtue of her sex.

Materialism

Torvald in particular focuses on money and material goods rather than people. His sense of manhood depends on his financial independence. He was an unsuccessful barrister because he refused to take "unsavory cases." As a result, he switched jobs to the bank, where he primarily deals with money. For him, money and materialism may be a way to avoid the complications of personal contact.

Children

Nora is called a number of diminutive, childlike names by Torvald throughout the play. These include "little songbird," "squirrel," "lark," "little featherhead," "little skylark," "little person," and "little woman." Torvald commonly uses the modifier "little" before the names he calls Nora. These are all usually followed by the possessive "my," signaling Torvald's belief that Nora is his. This pattern seems like more than just a collection of pet names. Overall, he sees Nora as a child of his.

The Helmer children themselves are only a borderline presence in the play, never given any dialogue to speak, and then only briefly playing hide-and-seek (perhaps a nod toward the theme of deception). Ibsen's alternate ending had Nora persuaded not to leave by the presence of the children. But the play as we have it does not really emphasize their importance. The story focuses on the parents.

Light

Light is used to illustrate Nora's personal journey. After the turning point of Torvald's claim to want to take everything upon himself and while Nora is talking to Dr. Rank, the light begins to grow dark just as Nora sinks to new levels of manipulation. When Dr. Rank reveals his affection, Nora is jolted out of this fantasy world into reality and insists on bringing a lamp into the room, telling the doctor that he must feel silly saying such things with the light on. Light, enlightenment, and shedding light on something all function as metaphors or idioms for understanding.

Dress and Costume

Nora's fancy dress for the party symbolizes the character she plays in her marriage to Torvald. Take note of when Nora is supposed to be wearing it and for whom. Note too that when she leaves Torvald in the last act, she first changes into different clothes, which suggests the new woman she is to become.

Religion

The play takes place around Christmas. The first act occurs on Christmas Eve, the second on Christmas Day, and the third on Boxing Day. Although there is a great deal of talk about morality throughout the play, Christmas is never presented as a religious holiday. Moreover, religion is directly questioned later by Nora in the third act. In fact, religion is discussed primarily as a material experience. Once again, what normally are important values for people and their relationships—children, personal contact, and, here, religion—are subordinate to materialism and selfish motives.

Corruption

Dr. Rank has inherited his tuberculosis from his father, who lived a morally questionable life, and in much the same way Nora worries that her morally reprehensible actions (fraudulently signing her father's name) will infect her children. Corruption, the play suggests, is hereditary. As he does in other plays, such as *The Wild Duck*, Ibsen explores the tension between real life and moral ideals.

The Life-Lie

Are you really alive, if, like Nora, you are living in a delusional world? This question resounds throughout Ibsen's canon, particularly in *The Wild Duck*, and the question is important in judging how to respond to the play. Is the end of the play, for instance, the glorious triumph of individualism, the moment at which Nora really becomes herself, or is it a foolish, idealistic decision which is the beginning of the end of Nora's happiness?

Glossary of Terms

dissolution

coming apart, as a person does during an illness

extravagant

luxurious; in excess of what is really necessary (especially in terms of cost or glamor).

feminism

the idea or ideal of gender equity in society, with a focus on issues pertaining to women.

flat

an apartment.

indiscreet

not discreet; not keeping a sensitive or delicate matter private.

IOU

a written document acknowledging a debt (as "I owe you...").

lament

to feel or express sorrow about a bad choice or bad circumstance.

lark

a songbird.

macaroon

a chewy, sweet cookie made with sugar and egg whites.

patronizing

condescending; expressing the idea that someone is lower than oneself.

spinal consumption

a disease something like tuberculosis, colloquially thought to be a consequence of the diminishment of semen. Nora says that Dr. Rank has the disease as a consequence of his father's misdeeds.

tarantella

a fast, whirling southern Italian dance, usually performed by a single couple, once supposed to be a remedy for a tarantula bite. This is the dance which Nora dances for Helmer at the party.

tuberculosis

a contagious wasting disease which causes chest pain and coughing up of blood. Untreated, it eventually is fatal.

Short Summary

A Doll's House traces the awakening of Nora Helmer from her previously unexamined life of domestic, wifely comfort. Having been ruled her whole life by either her father or her husband Torvald, Nora finally comes to question the foundation of everything she has believed in once her marriage is put to the test. Having borrowed money from a man of ill-repute named Krogstad by forging her father's signature, she was able to pay for a trip to Italy to save her sick husband's life (he was unaware of the loan, believing that the money came from Nora's father). Since then, she has had to contrive ways to pay back her loan, growing particularly concerned with money and the ways of a complex world.

When the play opens, it is Christmas Eve, and we find that Torvald has just been promoted to manager of the bank, where he will receive a huge wage and be extremely powerful. Nora is thrilled because she thinks that she will finally be able to pay off the loan and be rid of it. Her happiness, however, is marred when an angry Krogstad approaches her. He has just learned that his position at the bank has been promised to Mrs. Linde, an old school friend of Nora's who has recently arrived in town in search of work, and he tells Nora that he will reveal her secret if she does not persuade her husband to let him keep his position. Nora tries to convince Torvald to preserve Krogstad's job, using all of her feminine tricks (which he encourages), but she is unsuccessful. Torvald tells her that Krogstad's morally corrupt nature is physically repulsive to him and impossible to work with. Nora becomes very worried.

The next day, Nora is nervously moving about the house, afraid that Krogstad will appear at any minute. Her anxiety is reduced by being preoccupied with the preparations for a big fancy-dress party that will take place the next night in a neighbor's apartment. When Torvald returns from the bank, she again takes up her pleas on behalf of Krogstad. This time, Torvald not only refuses but also sends off the notice of termination that he has already prepared for Krogstad, reassuring a scared Nora that he will take upon himself any bad things that befall them as a result. Nora is extremely moved by this comment. She begins to consider the possibility of this episode transforming their marriage for the better—as well as the possibility of suicide.

Meanwhile, she converses and flirts with a willing Dr. Rank. Learning that he is rapidly dying, she has an intimate conversation with him that culminates in him professing his love for her just before she is able to ask him for financial help. His words stop her, and she steers the conversation back to safer ground. Their talk is interrupted by the announcement of Krogstad's presence. Nora asks Dr. Rank to leave and has Krogstad brought in.

Krogstad tells her that he has had a change of heart and that, though he will keep the bond, he will not reveal her to the public. Instead, he wants to give Torvald a note explaining the matter so that Torvald will be pressed to help Krogstad rehabilitate himself and keep his position at the bank. Nora protests against Torvald's involvement, but Krogstad drops the letter in Torvald's letterbox anyway, much to Nora's horror. Nora exclaims aloud that she and Torvald are lost. Still, she tries to use her charms to prevent Torvald from reading the letter, luring him away from business by begging him to help her with the tarantella for the next night's party. He agrees to put off business until the next day. The letter remains in the letterbox.

The next night, before Torvald and Nora return from the ball, Mrs. Linde and Krogstad, who are old lovers, reunite in the Helmers' living room. Mrs. Linde asks to take care of Krogstad and his children and to help him become the better man that he knows he is capable of becoming. The Helmers return from the ball as Mrs. Linde is leaving (Krogstad has already left), with Torvald nearly dragging Nora into the room. Alone, Torvald tells Nora how much he desires her but is interrupted by Dr. Rank. The doctor, unbeknownst to Torvald, has come by to say his final farewells, as he covertly explains to Nora. After he leaves, Nora is able to deter Torvald from pursuing her any more by reminding him of the ugliness of death that has just come between them, Nora having revealed Dr. Rank's secret. Seeing that Torvald finally has collected his letters, she resigns herself to committing suicide.

As she is leaving, though, Torvald stops her. He has just read Krogstad's letter and is enraged by its contents. He accuses Nora of ruining his life. He essentially tells her that he plans on forsaking her, contrary to his earlier claim that he would take on everything himself. During his tirade, he is interrupted by the maid bearing another note from Krogstad and addressed to Nora. Torvald reads it and becomes overjoyed. Krogstad has had a change of heart and has sent back the bond. Torvald quickly tells Nora that it is all over after all: he has forgiven her, and her pathetic attempt to help him has only made her more endearing than ever.

Nora, seeing Torvald's true character for the first time, sits her husband down to tell him that she is leaving him. After he protests, she explains that he does not love her—and, after tonight, she does not love him. She tells him that, given the suffocating life she has led until now, she owes it to herself to become fully independent and to explore her own character and the world for herself. As she leaves, she reveals to Torvald that she hopes that a "miracle" might occur: that one day, they might be able to unite in real wedlock. The play ends with the door slamming on her way out.

Summary and Analysis of Act I

It is Christmas Eve in the Helmer family's apartment, which is furnished "comfortably but not extravagantly." Nora enters with parcels, leaving a porter at the door with a Christmas tree, which she tells a maid to hide so that her children will not see it. She nibbles on some macaroons she has bought, but she hides them too when her husband, Torvald, comes out of his study. Torvald has recently been given a new job as a bank manager. Discussing her purchases with him, Nora is keen to spend more money, believing that her husband's new job will mean that the family no longer has to be careful with money.

In a series of complaints, Torvald chastises Nora for being a spendthrift, suggesting that she inherits the trait from her father. He points out that his new salary is not to be paid until April, and he wonders what would happen to her if he were to die before that time. He then gives her extra money to spend on presents, and he asks her what she would like as a Christmas gift. She asks for money. Torvald reminds her of the previous Christmas, when Nora apparently locked herself in a room to surprise everyone with homemade ornaments, which the cat then tore to bits. Torvald then asks her if she has bought any sweets or cakes in town—she lies and says no.

Nora is talking about Christmas again when the maid interrupts, announcing two visitors: an unknown woman, who is shown into the (onstage) living room, and Dr. Rank, who is shown into Torvald's study via a door (offstage). Torvald exits to his study, and Nora greets the stranger, whom she eventually recognizes as Mrs. Christine Linde, a friend from school whom she has not seen for almost a decade. Mrs. Linde is a widow. She tells Nora she feels that she has become much older. She had married her husband, not for love, but to provide financial and domestic security to her bedridden mother and her two younger brothers. Her mother has died and her brothers are adults, so she is now free to make her own life. But since her husband died penniless, she has had to work extremely hard for the past few years in order to support her relatives. In the course of this conversation about their lives since they last met, Nora mentions Torvald's new job and Mrs. Linde reveals that she came to see the Helmers to try to get a job from Torvald at the bank.

Mrs. Linde makes an offhand remark about how little Nora has had to worry about in life. She even calls Nora a child. Nora responds that she and Torvald both have had to work very hard to fund the life they have. In fact, she reports, early in their marriage, Torvald fell ill, and the doctor insisted that he must take a very costly vacation to Italy in order to recover. Since Torvald refused to borrow money, Nora borrowed it secretly, pretending it had come from her father. She has managed, secretly, to pay the quarterly installments and interest over the years. Nora now hopes that Torvald's new job will provide her with enough money to pay off the debts entirely.

Returning to the present, Nora happily reports that Torvald has been in good health ever since their trip. Mrs. Linde asks Nora whether she ever plans to tell Torvald. Nora replies that she may someday do so, if her good looks and charm wear off and she is in need of some way to keep Torvald's interest in her—but not yet.

The doorbell rings, and the maid informs Nora that Krogstad, who works at the bank, desires to see Torvald. Krogstad had loaned Nora the money, so she is shocked and worried that Krogstad has come to inform Torvald of the secret. She asks Krogstad about his business visiting them. Krogstad assures her that he comes only on bank business. When Krogstad goes into the study, Dr. Rank comes out to chat with Nora and Mrs. Linde.

Dr. Rank discusses with them the human urge to sustain life. He grudgingly admits that he wants to preserve his own life despite the physical pain his disease causes him. He then begins to discuss moral corruption, denouncing Krogstad as his immediate example.

Nora suddenly bursts out laughing. Not explaining herself to Mrs. Linde or Dr. Rank, she asks if the employees of the bank will be under the power of Torvald after his promotion. She revels in the idea. Still happy, she offers a macaroon to Dr. Rank. She claims that the macaroons were a gift from Mrs. Linde. Nora then impulsively shares with Mrs. Linde and Dr. Rank that there is something that she would very much like to say if Torvald were able to hear: "Bloody hell!" Her companions' reactions are cut short by the emergence of Torvald from the study.

Having dispatched Krogstad, Torvald returns to the living room. Nora immediately asks him to give Mrs. Linde employment, and Torvald suggests that he can probably get her a job. Nora reminds Dr. Rank and Mrs. Linde that they are expected to return the same evening, and as Dr. Rank exits with Torvald, a nurse shows in the three children. While they are engrossed in a game of hide-and-seek, Krogstad knocks and half enters the room. The game abruptly stops when his presence is recognized. Nora, somewhat shocked, sends the children out to the nurse and speaks to Krogstad.

Krogstad asks whether Mrs. Linde has been given an appointment at the bank. Nora confirms this and cautions Krogstad to be careful about offending Torvald, for Krogstad will be Torvald's subordinate at the bank. Krogstad then asks Nora to use her influence to ensure that he will be able to keep his position at the bank. Nora is confused and explains that she has no influence on such matters. In response, Krogstad reveals that he is prepared to fight for his position at the bank as if for his life, implying that he will not hesitate to reveal Nora's secret. Krogstad explains that his reputation at the bank, sullied by an indiscretion in the distant past, is extremely important to him and his social respectability. He threatens again to reveal Nora's secret. Nora then vehemently responds that he can do his worst. At this, Krogstad reveals that he knows that Nora, by signing her father's signature and dating it three days after his death, committed fraud in order to secure her loan. Nora refuses to believe that any court of law would convict her of a crime she committed only in order to save her husband's life. Krogstad leaves, still threatening to reveal what he knows.

When Krogstad leaves, Nora's children enter. Nora tells them not to mention Krogstad's visit to Torvald. She also reneges on her earlier promise to play with them, shooing them away. Nora begins to decorate the Christmas tree, and Torvald enters, asking what Krogstad came for. Nora asks about the nature of Krogstad's past indiscretion, and Torvald reveals that it was forgery. He condemns Krogstad in strong terms for failing to admit it. Torvald admits that he would have forgiven the man had Krogstad owned up to his lie. He suggests that such moral hypocrisy would even infect Krogstad's family. Torvald makes Nora promise never to plead Krogstad's case again. He also reveals his intention to fire Krogstad from the bank. Torvald exits to his study. Nora will not allow the children to come into the same room with her. Prompted by Torvald's comments about moral corruption over forgeries, she is terrified that she will "infect" her own children.

Analysis

In the tradition of the time, well-made plays used the first act as an exposition, the second to treat an event, and the third to unravel the issue. Ibsen will diverge from the pattern in the third act, but here the beginning is traditional, establishing the tensions that will explode later in the play. Ibsen sets up the act by introducing the central topic, Nora's character.

Specifically, the topic is Nora's relation to the home or the world outside the home. Nora is a symbol of the women of her time, who were thought to be content with the luxuries of modern society without worrying about the men's world outside the home. Many women were, but others were not, both as a matter of interest and as a matter of principle. Nora does delight in material wealth; Torvald is not entirely wrong in labeling her a spendthrift from an early age. She projects the attitude that money is the key to happiness. The issue is not quite so simple, though, for Nora's one great expense was to serve her husband's need to travel far from home for the sake of his health.

Nora already demonstrates some personal complexity, but generally she seems to have a fairly simplistic interaction with the outside world. This pattern is not entirely her fault, for she has not had any real opportunity to take her chances there. She moved from her father's home to her husband's. Torvald's treatment of Nora as a small, helpless child exacerbates Nora's isolation from reality.

In this context, note that a doll's house is a child's toy that often allows children to play at being adults. The exterior world, moreover, never makes it onto the stage. Nora is the doll in the house, and the house is the only location we see. Torvald controls the stage on which Nora is an actor who generally believes that this pretend-world is the real one. Just as Nora relates to the exterior world primarily through material objects, Torvald relates to Nora as an object that is possessed, a doll to be controlled within a small sphere.

Torvald's attitude pervades every word he speaks to Nora, and his objectification of her is most evident in his diminutive pet names for her. She is his little "lark" and "squirrel" and, later, his "songbird." Similarly, Torvald repeatedly calls Nora his "little one" or "little girl," maintaining the atmosphere of subordination more appropriate to a father than a husband. As for Nora, we see in this first conversation that she seems entirely dependent on Torvald for her money, her food, and her shelter, despite the fact that she is keeping a secret. This secret is the kernel of her individuality and her escape from the doll's house.

Nora's skewed vision of the world is most evident in her interactions with Mrs. Linde. Whereas her old school friend is wizened and somber, Nora is impetuous. Her choice to tell Mrs. Linde about her secret seems to be more the boast of a child than the actions of a thoughtful adult, and Mrs. Linde also refers to her as a child. Nora's naïve view of the law—that the law would not prosecute a forgery carried out in the name of a good purpose like love—reinforces the idea that Nora is fundamentally unaware of the ways of the real world.

Still, it is apparent that Nora is at least partly aware that her doll-like life is not the only choice. When pressed about whether she will ever tell Torvald about the loan, she replies that she will, in time. For now, she believes that telling him would upset the balance in her home. Torvald's position as the manly provider and lawgiver is something that she is willing to manipulate, at least from within the home. She knows that other women, like Mrs. Linde, have different levels of freedom and autonomy. It is important to examine the language of the opening scene between Nora and Torvald in this context. Nora's words could be partly sincere and partly insincere; the text suggests an ambiguity in Nora's awareness of her situation. This ambiguity is perhaps why Nora's character is so popular for actors to play; actors can use gesture and voice inflection to signal the true level of Nora's satisfaction with her sheltered place in the home and in Torvald's life.

Nevertheless, she does not seem want to face the implications of a choice to escape her confinement. She believes that material wealth will render her "free from care," allowing her not just to repay the debt but also to play with her children, keep the house beautifully, and do everything the way that Torvald likes. The lie about the loan can be preserved. She seems content with her one great secret, her knowledge that she has done something for Torvald entirely without prompting from him. When Mrs. Linde complains that she feels unspeakably empty without anyone to care for, Nora can feel some comfort in her domestic situation with children and a husband, and this ideal of domestic tranquility is reiterated throughout the text.

It is a happy first act for the family, but Krogstad's presence launches the crisis that will consume Nora's attention. The family seems functional, the room is comfortable, and Nora seems to have the Christmas spirit (for instance, she generously tips the porter who brings in the Christmas tree). The family seems to be, as Aristotle might have had it, at the height of happiness—from which they will tumble downhill. Nora's secret, which might come out before its time, puts an ominous cloud over the doll's house. The outside world now invades the home in the form of Mrs. Linde and then Krogstad. These machinations about who should get the banking jobs, complicated by Krogstad's threat to reveal the secret and by Torvald's denunciation of Krogstad, are just too much for Nora to manage.

Perhaps the coldness of the Norwegian winter in which the play is set represents the coolness, societal conformity, and comfortable routine of Nora's world. In contrast is a kind of repressed Italy—referenced most obviously in Nora's outfit and the tarantella—featuring heat, passion, truth, desire, and the flame of individuality. Nora's secret is bound to come out. Ibsen has set up an ironic inevitability. All who know are waiting for the moment at which the lie falls apart. Torvald almost is cuckolded by the lie.

Summary and Analysis of Act II

Act II occurs in the same room as Act I. The Christmas tree's decorations have been taken down, and the candles have burned out. Nora is alone, anxiously worrying about whether Krogstad will write to Torvald revealing her secret. She is interrupted by the Nurse, who brings in a box of fancy clothes to look at. Nora asks about her children and hints at negative events to come, telling the Nurse that Nora will not be able to be with her children as much as before. When the Nurse replies that the children will cope with her absence, Nora wonders aloud if they would forget her altogether if she were to go away. The Nurse is shocked.

Nora asks her how the Nurse could have felt comfortable leaving her own children among strangers when she first came to nurse Nora, when Nora was only a child. The Nurse replies that she was grateful for such a good position and that, given her financial situation, she could not pass up the opportunity. Nora tells the Nurse what a wonderful mother she has been for Nora—and she would be a wonderful mother to Nora's children if they were suddenly without a mother. The Nurse exits.

Alone again, Nora unsuccessfully tries to concentrate on the party being held that night in the upstairs flat, so that she could forget the problem of Krogstad revealing her secret. She is interrupted by Mrs. Linde's arrival. Mrs. Linde enquires about Dr. Rank's depressive mood the day before, and Nora explains that Dr. Rank suffers from a very dangerous spinal tuberculosis that he has had from childhood. Nora hints that Dr. Rank's problem is the result of his father's sexual indiscretions.

Mrs. Linde quietly continues to inquire about Nora's relationship with Dr. Rank and wonders if he is Nora's "rich admirer." Nora replies that Dr. Rank is a family friend and that there is no such admirer. Mrs. Linde pursues her idea, calls Dr. Rank tactless, and presumes that he is the one from whom Nora borrowed the money. Hearing Torvald approaching, Nora does not answer and bustles Mrs. Linde into another room in order to hide the fancy-dress costume from him.

Torvald and Nora discuss her dress. As he leaves, Nora stops him and asks him repeatedly if he would do something for his "little squirrel" or "skylark" if she were to act very "prettily," dancing and singing for him. Nora asks him to reconsider dismissing Krogstad from the bank, but Torvald becomes angry, revealing that it is Krogstad's post that he has promised to Mrs. Linde. Nora tells Torvald that she fears Krogstad who, once dismissed, will attempt to besmirch their name in the newspapers.

Torvald thinks that Nora is afraid of libel because her father's name was sullied in the newspapers after his death, so he reassures Nora that, unlike her father, he is beyond reproach. Nora warns about the contrivances of men like Krogstad against their happy, family home. Torvald finally replies that Nora's pleas make it all the more impossible for him to change his mind. What if word got out that he had reversed his decision simply because of his wife's anxieties? Torvald argues that Krogstad is taking advantage of their early childhood friendship to speak to him in an inappropriately familiar manner, which would make his position as manager intolerable. Incredulous, Nora tells Torvald that he surely must not be so narrow-minded. Becoming ever more angry, Torvald orders the maid to send Krogstad his letter of dismissal at once.

To calm Nora, who is panicking, Torvald assures her that, come what may, he will have the courage to take upon himself anything and everything that happens. Nora is particularly intrigued and horrified by this statement, so she asks Torvald to clarify it. He simply repeats that he will take upon himself everything that comes their way. Nora states that this will never happen. Torvald interprets her statement as a desire to share the burdens as husband and wife and assures her that this is what he has in mind as well. He then dismisses the whole topic, asking her if she feels better and telling her to go back to practicing her dancing for the next night's ball. He also instructs her to direct Dr. Rank to his study, leaving her alone. His tone is that of a father figure.

Nora is bewildered with anxiety until she is interrupted by the arrival of Dr. Rank. Nora detains him and tells him that she always has time for him. Dr. Rank replies in kind. Confused by his statement, Nora asks him to clarify his interests, asking him if anything is likely to happen between them. Dr. Rank reveals that he expects to be dead within a month. He then asks Nora to prevent Torvald from entering Rank's sickroom once he has entered the final stages of his disease. He arranges to leave Nora a visiting card with a black cross on it at the right time to signify that he is about to die. As night approaches, Nora and Rank have an odd conversation which flits between the serious and the mildly flirtatious. For instance, Nora pulls out a pair of silk stockings to show him, and they talk about how much leg Nora will have to show him for him to form an opinion about the stockings.

Nora is clearly building up toward asking Dr. Rank for financial help. He then, seemingly unexpectedly, confesses that he loves Nora. He says that he only visits the household on her account. This confession makes her request for money impossible, for it now would make their relationship tangled and explicit. Nora leaves the room briefly to bring in a lamp. Steering the conversation back to safer territory, Nora explains why she loves Torvald even though she seems to enjoy her time with Dr. Rank more. She observes the similarities between her relationships with Torvald and with her deceased father.

The maid enters with Krogstad's visiting card, telling Nora that he has refused to leave until he has seen Nora. Dr. Rank finally retires to Torvald's study. When Krogstad enters, Nora tells him to speak low, warning him that Torvald is home. Krogstad, unperturbed, asks her for an explanation for his dismissal from the bank. Nora replies that she did her best pleading his case but could not sway her husband. Assuming that Nora told Torvald everything, Krogstad replies that Torvald must love her very little to have made such a decision. Nora informs him that Torvald still knows nothing about the matter. Krogstad asks her if she now has a clearer idea of what she has done, and Nora replies that she does, very well. Krogstad now replies that he will not make the matter public after all, but he will keep it between Nora, himself, and Torvald. Nora protests that Torvald must not know, but Krogstad replies that, even if she did have the money to pay the outstanding balance on the loan, he would still involve Torvald, for his intention is not to expose Nora but to blackmail Torvald. That is, he now intends to use Nora's IOU to pressure Torvald into giving him a new, highly-placed job at the bank. Krogstad exits and drops a letter to Torvald into the locked letter-box to which only Torvald has a key.

Mrs. Linde returns, and Nora reveals her problem, asking her friend to be her witness in case anything should befall Nora. Nora insists that, in such a case, Mrs. Linde should tell everyone that Nora was not insane and, more importantly, was completely responsible for everything. Mrs. Linde responds in confusion, and Nora asserts that Mrs. Linde could never understand the "miracle" that is about to happen. This miracle, Nora elaborates, is "frightening," yet it "mustn't happen, not for anything in the world."

Mrs. Linde offers to try to convince Krogstad to retrieve the letter—she would use her old amorous connection with him as a method of persuasion. Nora says that it is hopeless. But when Torvald begins knocking on the door, Mrs. Linde resolves to try and exits quickly. Nora unlocks the door for Torvald and Dr. Rank, but they are surprised because they expected Nora to be trying on her dress; Torvald says that Rank has been preparing him "for some great transformation scene." Torvald observes instead that Nora looks worn out and asks her if she has been practicing her dancing too much. Nora replies that she could not even do so without Torvald because she cannot remember anything without him. Hoping to distract him long enough to solve the problem with the letter, she asks him to help her all day and night until the party. Torvald agrees.

But he heads toward the letter-box first, so Nora stops him by playing the first bars of the tarantella she is going to dance. She then lures him to play for her and correct her while she dances. Dr. Rank, until now an observer, eventually takes over at the piano so Torvald can stand and correct Nora better. Her dancing grows more wild and desperate until her hair has all come undone. While Nora is still dancing, Mrs. Linde returns and observes that she is dancing like her life depended on it.

Torvald eventually calls everything to a halt, chastising Nora for having forgotten everything he has taught her. Nora replies that she has indeed forgotten everything and needs his help to relearn the dance. She tells him that he must not think of anything else, especially not any letters. Torvald remarks that he can tell from her behavior that there is a letter from Krogstad waiting for him. Nora responds that she does not know, but that there might be. She implores him not to let anything horrible come between them until after the party. Torvald takes her into his arms, calling her a child and agreeing that she must have her way. He promises to work with her until after the party—at which point, in Nora's words, he "will be free."

They all retire to dinner. Nora calls for lots of macaroons. As they leave, Torvald and Dr. Rank exchange a few words about Nora's state of mind in a way that makes clear that they have discussed this matter before. Dr. Rank, concerned, asks if Nora is expecting something (the text is ambiguous—maybe a child, maybe just the possible letter). Torvald finally dismisses her concerning behavior as evidence of childish nervousness, and they exit.

Alone with Nora, Mrs. Linde tells Nora that Krogstad has gone out of town. Nora seems unconcerned and refers again to the miracle. Mrs. Linde presses Nora to explain herself, but Nora dismisses her questions, telling her she would not understand. She sends Mrs. Linde into the dining room. Now alone, she composes herself, checks the time, and observes that she has thirty-one hours to live (that is, until after the tarantella). Torvald's voice then rings out; he is asking for his "little skylark." The act ends with Nora going to him "with her arms wide."

Analysis

Act I set up the initial invasion of reality into Nora's world and the first disruptions to the basic underpinnings of Nora's life. Her assumption of the roles of wife and mother seemed comfortable enough even if the roles rested on fragile premises. Act II eventually sees Nora set up a test that will determine whether or not her domestic world is false to her basic nature. That is, having been confronted with the fact that Torvald will find out about her lie, the test is whether or not the discovery of her secret will strengthen or dissolve the marriage. If Torvald is really the loving husband she wishes he were, his discovery will only strengthen their marriage. The alternative is some kind of miracle that will free both of them from the iron cage of marriage that is expected of them. Her reaction to Krogstad's finally dropping his letter in the box is the climax of the play. This step will lead inevitably in one direction or the other, but we are not sure which way it will go. Since the play has not seemed so much like a comedy so far, we can predict that the revelations in the letter will turn out badly and that the idea of a miracle has more to do with a suicide.

Nora is still trying to confront the fact that her world can be touched and shattered. Though she is shaken at the prospect of the revelations, before it is too late she still believes that her family and her material comforts might protect her. Even before it is too late, however, she is worried enough that she has already begun to consider the ideas of running away or committing suicide (though she admits that she does not have the perverse courage for this).

Luckily, the planning for the party temporarily distracts her. This party is extremely important for Nora because, through the costumes and dance, she is able to keep up the hope (or pretense) that the basic elements of her relationship with Torvald are still intact. She is literally wearing a costume and playing a role, not much different from what she does every day. Mrs. Linde refers to Nora's dress as her "fine feathers," reinforcing the general idea that Nora has been something other than an independent human.

In fact, the dress is a potent symbol of Nora's character. Like Nora, it is torn and in need of repair. As in real life, Nora feels she is incapable of fixing the problem herself, giving the dress to Mrs. Linde to mend. Nora likewise reports that Torvald dislikes seeing dressmaking in action, suggesting that Torvald enjoys the false character that Nora has adopted but has no desire to see the real Nora before she reconstructs herself to fulfill her expected roles. To complete the working out of this line of symbolism, in the final act Nora will remove the dress and effectively unmask herself so that, pretense aside, she and Torvald will meet as humans together for the first time.

The theme of parenthood and children is interestingly explored in the conversation between Nora and the nurse at the beginning of the act. We have already seen the odd child-parent dynamic that sometimes exists between Torvald and Nora. Here Ibsen seems to imply that the nurse has raised Nora's three children precisely as she raised Nora. Her period of childhood has never really ended, for her nurse is still with her. One of the oddities of the play is the apparent ease with which Nora will finally abandon her children. They seem not to be central to her life with (or without) Torvald.

It has often been noted that Dr. Rank's physical disease represents the spread of moral corruption, for his disease apparently has been inherited from his morally questionable father, who kept mistresses. This coupling of moral corruption with its physical manifestation was treated in the first act, when Nora worried that her moral corruption in forging her father's signature might "infect" her children. Ibsen's visual language during Nora's conversation with Dr. Rank—the darkening of day into night until it is so dark that Nora has to leave for a lamp (though this also gives her a break from the difficult conversation)—potently expresses the moral corruption which pervades the characters in the play.

Of course, in their conversation, Nora seems to be considering whether she should exploit Rank's at first unspoken desire for her in order to gain his money. Yet, interestingly, the moment the lamp is switched on and Rank confesses his love for Nora, Nora's plan falls apart. When there is no direct risk of an illicit romantic relationship, she can work her charms to ask a great favor, but once the cat is out of the bag, Nora cannot involve herself with Rank financially because of the romantic complications that would ensue.

Again, Nora's hopes of averting disaster are dashed when she sees Krogstad drop the letter into Torvald's box. She has perceived that there have been problems in their relationship, so she exclaims that all is lost as Krogstad deposits the letter. She guesses that Torvald will not pass the test. The letter-box itself becomes a rich symbol of concealment and revelation. Her primary attention turns to the box and keeping Torvald from it for as long as possible. Nora's fear, now that she knows that there is no turning back, is that the "miracle" will happen. Maybe Torvald will try to take this all upon himself. He even says that he will, at one point, and this gives Nora some moments of hope. Maybe, knowing what she has done for him, they will become equal partners in the marriage. Nora both fears this and wishes for it even though she is preparing, prudently, for the worst.

Still, Nora is not ready to face this test yet. Delaying the inevitable (she knows that Mrs. Linde's efforts will be fruitless), she wants to act out her last chance to be a doll-creature for Torvald. There is still a chance things will work out, so she must keep up appearances for at least a little while longer, and she might be happy enough to stay in her domestic roles after all. But the pressure of uncertainty is too much for now. She dances the tarantella wildly, as though she really is shaking off the poison of the tarantula bite.

This casting off of cares shakes her up enough to turn to the idea of Torvald's and Nora's separate freedom. It is only after the dancing that she consents to letting him be free. Interestingly, her statement that she only has thirty-one hours to live can be read two different ways. On the one hand, it can be interpreted as saying that she plans on committing suicide in order to free Torvald from having to take the responsibility for the debt upon himself. She would die knowing that she had once again saved his life. On the other hand, it may be a metaphorical death; her life as she knows it will be over and she soon will be embarking on a new, radically different life course because her relationship with Torvald will be over. But in either case, there is still the matter of Krogstad's planned blackmail of Torvald. Will this be at all her problem, though, once she has escaped from her life with Torvald? Her escape from her artificial domestic life will entail escape from her real responsibilities as well.

Summary and Analysis of Act III

The act opens in the same room on the next night, Boxing Day. Mrs. Linde is absentmindedly trying to read. As the sounds of dance music suggest, Torvald and Nora are upstairs at the party. Mrs. Linde is waiting for Krogstad so that she can talk to him about Nora's situation. When Krogstad arrives, he and Mrs. Linde turn almost immediately to a discussion of why Mrs. Linde jilted him (for her now-deceased husband) many years ago. Mrs. Linde explains that, though she has questioned her decision many times, she had to pursue her former husband's money given that her mother and brothers depended on her to survive. Krogstad reveals that her departure left him "a shipwrecked man clinging to a spar." Mrs. Linde replies that she is now in his position and that she longs for them to come together. She tells him that he is the reason that she came to town. She still wants a family to look after.

The music of the tarantella is heard above, and Mrs. Linde urges Krogstad to be quick. Krogstad now grows suspicious, questioning whether she is saying all of this simply on behalf of Nora. She denies it, and he then offers to take the letter back. She now urges him not to, admitting that this had been her original intention after all. She explains that, since her first discovery of the problem the day before, she has witnessed enough in the house to convince her that Torvald must read the letter. The Helmers need a "full understanding" of their situation in order to maintain a successful marriage. Krogstad leaves, promising Mrs. Linde that he will meet her in a few minutes. Hearing Nora and Torvald coming, Mrs. Linde prepares to leave, commenting on what a difference having people to care for makes in her life.

The Helmers appear in costume: Nora is a Neapolitan fisher-girl, and Torvald is in evening wear and a black coat. Torvald is bringing Nora into the room almost by force. She is trying to get him to return to the party upstairs. Torvald refuses, citing their earlier agreement. They greet Mrs. Linde, who explains that she stayed up in order to see Nora in her dress. Torvald brags about how lovely Nora looks, describing his wife's successful evening. He tells Mrs. Linde that Nora danced the tarantella marvelously—even if her performance was "a trifle too realistic." He tried to make her exit equally artistic by ushering her around the room for a last bow and then disappearing into the night, but Nora did not appreciate his exit attempts. "An exit," Torvald claims, "should always be dramatic." Torvald then leaves to light some candles and air out the house a bit, giving Nora a chance to ask Mrs. Linde for news from Krogstad. Mrs. Linde says that Nora must tell Torvald everything. Nora is not shocked; she simply thanks Mrs. Linde for telling her, and she now knows what she must do.

Torvald returns and Mrs. Linde soon leaves. Nora then asks Torvald if he is tired, telling him that she is quite sleepy. Torvald replies that he is quite awake and has been waiting to be alone with his wife all evening. He calls her beautiful and fascinating, his "treasured possession." He observes that she must still have the alluring tarantella in her blood. He launches into an explanation of why he pretends not to know her at parties: it is his fantasy about meeting and seducing her for the first time. He likes to feel that she is his new bride about to be his for the first time. Nora tries to push him off, much to his confusion and displeasure.

They are interrupted by Dr. Rank. The three talk about the ball and all its finery. Unknown to Torvald, Dr. Rank reveals to Nora through his conversation that he will soon die. Dr. Rank eventually leaves, and Nora calls to him, "Sleep well." Torvald begins to head out to empty the mailbox so that the newspapers can be delivered in the morning. Nora unsuccessfully tries to stop him. At the mailbox, Torvald is surprised to find that someone has tried to pick the lock with one of Nora's hairpins. Nora tells him that it must have been one of the children.

Torvald is surprised to find two visiting cards from Dr. Rank with black crosses just above his name. Torvald comments on the gruesomeness of the mark, and Nora confirms that he has used it to announce his death. Torvald thinks it might be "best this way," for now he and his wife have only each other. Torvald embraces Nora, telling her how much he cares for her. He wishes that he could somehow save her from some great danger so that he could risk everything for her sake. Nora disengages herself from his embrace. She tells him with resolution that he must now read his letters; she no longer is delaying the inevitable but is avoiding his advances. Torvald agrees that something ugly has come between them—he believes it is because of the news of Dr. Rank—and that it would be best to spend the night apart. They separate, and Torvald goes off to read his letters.

Alone, Nora prepares to rush off to commit suicide by jumping into the icy depths of the river, throwing on Torvald's coat and her shawl. As she bids adieu to her family and rushes out the door, Torvald hurries out of his room and stops her, letter in hand. Torvald asks her if she knows what is in the letter, but Nora still tries to leave. He stops her, locking the door. He continues to wonder out loud how the letter's allegations could be true. He dismisses her pleas that all was done out of love. He protests that he will not suffer at her hands.

Nora realizes that Torvald has no intention of taking the burden of this problem upon himself; he is blaming her for ruining his life. She grows still and cold while Torvald berates her and her character. Not allowing Nora to speak, Torvald speculates about their future. They will keep up appearances but, of course, Nora will not be allowed near the children and the normal aspects of their marriage will no longer be maintained in private.

He is interrupted by the maid, who is bearing a note from Krogstad to Nora. Torvald intercepts the letter and reads it himself, learning that Krogstad has had a change of heart and has sent back the bond after all. Torvald is overjoyed and shouts, "I am saved!" Nora asks whether she is saved as well, and he says yes since "nobody has any hold over you." Overcome with relief, he now discusses how hard this all must have been for Nora and tells her that he has forgiven her—he will think of it only as a bad dream. It is all over.

Realizing perhaps that Nora is not having the same reaction, Torvald explains to her that he knows that she did everything out of love and that he can forgive her because he also knows that, as a woman, she is unequipped to make proper decisions. He even tells her that her helplessness and full dependency on him make her all the more endearing to him. Nora thanks him for his forgiveness and leaves the room to take off her ball dress.

As she is removing her dress, Torvald stands in the doorway and muses about the comfort of their home and how much he wants to and will protect her. He assures her that everything will soon be as it was before. The helplessness of a wife makes her even more attractive because she becomes both a wife and child, doubly his own. Moreover, when the husband forgives her, he gives her new life and becomes even closer to her.

The change of heart apparently rings hollow. Nora changes not into bed clothing but into everyday clothing. She explains that she will not sleep tonight, and she asks him to sit down with her in order to "face facts." She tells him that he has never understood her and that, before tonight, she has never understood him. She points out that, over eight years of marriage, they have never before sat down to have a serious discussion. Torvald protests that such conversations would not have made sense, given Nora's interests.

Nora tells him that she has been greatly wronged by both her father and her husband. Torvald protests that they are the men who have loved her the most. Shaking her head, Nora corrects him, telling him that he has never loved her for herself but has only thought it pleasant to be in love with her. She explains to him that, just as her father did, Torvald has treated her as a doll to be played with, arranging everything to suit himself and forcing her to live only to entertain him. As a result, she has not made anything of her life and has never been truly happy.

Torvald agrees with this analysis, though he qualifies it as exaggerated and strained. He pledges that, from now on, he will stop playing with her and start educating her. Nora refuses the offer, observing that he is not the man to educate her. Only a few minutes before, he had told her that she was unfit to raise her own children. She agrees with him about her inability at present; she must first educate herself before she can educate the children. This is why, she concludes, she is going to leave him.

Torvald is shocked and jumps out of his chair, calling her mad and trying to prevent her from leaving. He accuses her of neglecting her "most sacred duties" as wife and mother, refusing to acknowledge Nora's opinion that her duty to herself as a reasonable human being is at least as sacred. He appeals to her sense of religion and then morality, both of which Nora agnostically rejects by explaining that she has never had a chance to examine and embrace these things on her own and, as a result, she does not know if she agrees with these principles. He finally argues that he must conclude that she does not love him. Apologetic, she agrees. He lost her love earlier tonight (if not before), and she cannot stay in the house.

Nora explains that her love was lost because the miracle did not happen: he did not refuse Krogstad's conditions and offer to take up the problem for himself. Instead, he berated her. Torvald replies that, though he would gladly work day and night for her, he would never assent to jeopardizing his honor for a loved one. Nora simply replies that many wives have done just that. Torvald dismisses her words as those of a heedless child. Admitting the possibility that he might be right, Nora changes tack. She describes his selfish perspective and her own horror at having realized that she had lived with and borne children with a stranger for eight years. Torvald sadly acknowledges the gulf between them but asks if there is still a way to fill it. Nora reiterates that they both will be better off apart. She somewhat formally releases him from all obligations to her. She says that there must be perfect freedom on both sides. They return their wedding rings to each other, and she leaves her keys.

Nora adds that a future relationship of some sort would only be possible if "the miracle of miracles" were to happen—if they both change is such a way that they could have a real marriage. She leaves. Sinking down into a chair with his hand in his face, Torvald moans her name. He then looks up and observes how empty the room has become without her. The play ends with the hope of the "miracle of miracles" crossing Torvald's mind and with the sound of the street door slamming.

Analysis

This act elaborates on the deciding point of Nora's life. The test of whether the "miracle" happen or not is a test that will decide whether Torvald really is the husband he has claimed to be, whether the marriage really is salvageable in a way that will raise Nora out of the disrespect of being a doll. Nora has awoken to the reality that she is living a doll's life and needs to move on with her own life, with or without Torvald. Her new life has already begun, and we have little hope that Torvald will rise to the challenge anytime soon. We do not yet know, though, if Nora will choose to live or to commit suicide upon Torvald's likely failure in the test. One of the key reasons that the act works so successfully is that audiences feel the suspense about what will happen once Torvald reads the letter.

The relationship between Mrs. Linde and Krogstad makes for a good comparison with Nora's and Torvald's marriage. Mrs. Linde's and Krogstad's decision to be together after all this time is sincere, sweet, and reasonable, even if they are choosing somewhat traditional gender roles. Although Mrs. Linde and Krogstad both suffer from significant personal and moral problems, they might have a better chance of a happy and true marriage than Nora and Torvald had. Mrs. Linde advocates revealing all to Torvald because, as her union with Krogstad suggests, she believes that it is possible to build a relationship based upon mutual dependence so long as both parties are fully aware of each other's ideas and motives. Mrs. Linde hopes that, through her own new union, both she and Krogstad can eventually become the better people they know that they can be. This is a pattern for the "miracle of miracles," a mutual choice to change so that both parties are truly ready for a successful marriage. Given the history of Krogstad and Mrs. Linde, however, we cannot yet see this relationship working as well as they hope. Ibsen leaves the issue open. At least the quality of respect and communication between them is already far above the situation for Torvald and Nora. In addition, all the years of thinking about each other have given Krogstad and Mrs. Linde a special anticipation for one another. This is the opposite of the effect of the years of sourness that Nora now sees when she examines her marriage.

The extent of Torvald's investment in a fantasy world and the importance of his false characterization of Nora are revealed when he describes how, at parties, he pretends not to know her so that he may seduce her all over again. Perhaps more importantly, Nora is quite candid about her understanding of all this, telling him flatly that she knows. If she did not know before, she knows now. She is no longer willing to be an object or an agent of fantasy. If there is one thing she now knows, it is the difference between fantasy and reality.

This is a very recent development. She apparently has recently tried to pick the lock of Torvald's letter-box with one of her hairpins. In that effort she seems to have preferred the status quo, keeping the secret a bit longer. Perhaps Krogstad could be appeased and the secret could be held forever. But the effort failed, and Nora has had to accept the reality that she is not herself. The costume of the Neapolitan fisher-girl, with which she entered the scene, is a clear symbol of her own unreality. When she later changes into a plain black dress, we realize that she has shifted to a final acknowledgment of her new chance at an individual identity, free of Torvald.

It is important to notice that Nora's time at the party has been the first time that she has left the confines of the one room in the entire play. She is not far away, however. At this point, she has to be dragged back in. This is not merely an attempt to delay the reading of the letter; she longs to stay off the stage, to stay away from the doll's house where Torvald controls her. She would rather be in the delirium of the tarantella. She sees that a major element of the problem in their relationship is Torvald's desire to have Nora entertain him, so she is eager to try her luck in the real world and make her own choices. When she briefly leaves the room to exchange her party dress for everyday clothing, this is her first lone foray from the room. This step foreshadows her final departure. She is not going to go to some hotel, however; she might just kill herself, but if not, she will go to the home of a friend or to her earlier family home. She is not ready to be fully free; she needs a safe place to recollect herself, to get herself educated and ready to enter into a healthy marriage or, if she chooses, to find a room of her own.

When she finally leaves, she seems to have decided to move on positively with her life rather than to commit suicide. Before Torvald confronted her with the letter, she was thinking seriously commit suicide, determined that Torvald should not have to sacrifice his life for hers. She considered this an appropriate choice insofar as she thought that he would willingly give his life for hers when necessary. In this way, they would have had an equal relationship. But she became extremely disappointed to discover that he clearly had no intention of sacrificing himself for her. Instead of refusing to abide by Krogstad's demands and taking up the issue for himself, Torvald accused Nora of ruining his life. He even told her that this would conclude their marriage: she would no longer be allowed to see her children or maintain their marriage except in public appearances. He said he would never sacrifice his honor for a loved one. His emotional tirade was shameful. His reversal of all this, once Krogstad's threat had lifted, was equally selfish. This is not a man worth dying for.

Nora realizes that, before she can be a wife, she must first discover herself in the world. She leaves as an awakened soul, determined to become a full person rather than the doll of the male figures in her life. Thus, it is important to note that Nora's motives are not simply idealistic. She does not know yet whether she should adhere to religion or morality or virtue, but she knows that she must escape the oppressive situation in order to figure out what to do next.

The change in Helmer's expressed character probably does not dupe either Nora or the audience. He begins the act rather unsympathetically. His objectification of Nora extends so far as practically demanding to have sexual intercourse with her against her will. He belittles and berates her. He acts selfishly throughout. Yet, when left alone at the end with his children, plaintively begging that the gulf between him and his wife might be bridged, we recognize that he truly feels devastated. He believed the myth of their marriage with his whole heart. He, too, has been limited by the gender roles of husband and wife that his society tends to expect. This makes him hugely sympathetic despite his many serious failings and even despite his cruelty.

Ibsen manipulates the audience with several intimations of a happy ending: when Krogstad and Mrs. Linde's love is revealed, when Krogstad promises that he will take back his letter, when he returns Helmer's IOU, and when Nora and Torvald discuss the possibility of a "miracle of miracles." But the outside door slams as the curtain comes down. It is not a happy ending but a sad one, particularly for Torvald. There is only a remote possibility of the redemption of the Helmers' marriage. As for Nora, it is an open ending. It is an opening out of possibilities for Nora, a new journey which, as much as possible, she will take alone.

Suggested Essay Questions

1. **The play is usually considered one of Ibsen's "realist" plays. Consider how far the play might be anti-realist or symbolic.**

   Answer: Consider the symbols, metaphors, and imagery of the play, and weigh their importance against the elements that seem realistic. It also should be very helpful to define "realism" over against the uses of symbols and elements that are absurd, grotesque, or fantastic. Note that "realism" and "symbolism" have gained specific connotations within Ibsen criticism.
2. **When Nora says in Act One, "I can't think of anything to wear. It all seems so stupid and meaningless," Ibsen illustrates the symbolism of clothing in the play. Describe how Ibsen's use of clothing works in the play.**

   Answer: Consider, especially, Nora's tarantella costume and fancy-dress box, as well as her black dress when taking the clothing is a symbol. Explore the metaphor of clothing as something which covers up, something which disguises, or as something which confers identity. Ibsen also uses clothing to make points about agency and gender. Consider who dresses whom and who wears certain clothes for the sake of personal expression or in order to please someone else.
3. **Why is freedom important in the play?**

   Answer: Nora sees herself as not free when she is confined in the domestic life of her husband's home. The direction of the play is to perceive Nora's awakening as someone who deserves freedom. Consider, too, that Torvald becomes free of his marriage obligations, which also have been oppressive of his own liberties. Finally, consider the ambiguous nature of the freedom Nora wins. She is going from a fairly predictable life into something unknown. Remember that Mrs. Linde would rather be tied to a family rather than alone and on her own. Is that because of human nature or because of her individual choice?
4. **Is Torvald Helmer a deeply abhorrent character?**

   Answer: To answer this question, perform a detailed character study of Torvald Helmer. Do not jump to a conclusion based on your initial feelings about his words and actions in the play. Weigh both sides of the argument—what specifically is the problem in the marriage and in his choices? If you decide to abhor the character, how bad is he? Consider the ways in which he genuinely loves his wife, earns money for the household, and pays attention to her against his selfishness, oppression of his wife, and ability to handle stress.
5. **How does the play illustrate inheritance, the passing along of traits from parent to child?**

Answer: Consider Dr. Rank's illness as attributed to his father's indiscretions. Krogstad's shame for his own alleged errors is inherited by his children by way of reputation. Consider, most of all, Nora's relationships with her father and her nurse as influences on how she treats her own children.

6. **What is the importance of the title of the play?**

   Answer: This is a reasonably straightforward question that could be taken in a number of directions. How far is Nora a doll, an object or toy for others? How does her home represent a doll's house, from which the doll cannot escape on her own? When Nora leaves the house, she is breaking free of the metaphor, though it is unclear what will happen if she is going to return to her earlier family home, where she was something of a doll to her father.

7. **Ibsen once described Mrs Alving in his play *Ghosts* as a version of Nora in later life. Imagine what Nora's earlier life might have been like, based on her characterization in the play.**

   Answer: If up till the last day, Nora has been living in a fantasy world, she must have been even less self-aware or independent when she was younger. She probably married by being enthralled by her society's ideas of love and marriage. Under her father and nurse, she seems to have had few opportunities to get anything like a liberal education; instead, she seems to have learned only how to be a traditional girl and a traditional woman.

8. **To what extent is the play a comedy?**

   Answer: As well as considering smaller touches, such as individual lines, or jokes that might be funny or comedic, it is worth learning about the theatrical definitions of comedy and tragedy to consider how the structure of the play and the main plot elements might count as part of the tradition of comedy. Consider the roles of marriage, death, friendship, self-awareness, irony, family, holidays and parties, and the various themes of the play in this context.

9. **Is *A Doll's House* a feminist play?**

   Answer: Ibsen claimed that his play was about liberation in a more general, human sense, rather than specifically about female liberation. If feminism focuses on both men and women, it is reasonable to see the mutual liberation of Torvald and Nora as a feminist goal, liberating people of both sexes from social and cultural limitations based on gender. Consider the various women in the play as well. How are we to know whether Ibsen wants us to approve or disapprove of their various choices in relation to men and to their own goals? How do the characters themselves exhibit any goals or points that could be described as feminist?

10. **How does Ibsen provide suspense in the play?**

Answer: The audience wonders when Torvald will read the letter and what will happen when he does. We also do not know if Nora is going to decide to kill herself, leave, or stay home, but we do know that the pressure on her is building and that something in her is going to burst. Foreshadowing contributes to these issues, such as when Nora tells Mrs. Linde that she has plans Mrs. Linde cannot understand.

11. **Compare the relationship between Mrs. Linde and Krogstad with that of Nora and Torvald.**

    Answer: Nora and Torvald have lived in something of a fantasy marriage for years, and finally they are separating. Meanwhile, Mrs. Linde and Krogstad have been apart, thinking about one another, and finally they are getting together with a larger degree of self-understanding and maturity.

A Performance History of the Play

The world premiere of *A Doll's House* (*Et dukkehjem*) took place at the Royal Theatre in Copenhagen on December 21, 1879. The premiere date was fitting for the Christmastime setting of the play. Two weeks earlier, a print run of 8,000 copies of the script had been published, and it already had sold out. Some critics likely had read the text well in advance of the production. The production, largely naturalistic, retained a symmetrical arrangement of furniture along the walls, giving perhaps a slightly abstracted feel. Betty Hennings was the first Nora, and the production was directed by H. P. Holst.

Contrary to popular belief, word spread reasonably slowly about the play. It was two years before the play was performed outside Scandinavia and Germany, and ten years before a recognizably faithful version was seen in England or America. France did not see the play until 1894. By the time it took its place in the European theatre annals, Ibsen was over sixty.

The year 1880 saw the German production of *A Doll's House* starring a well-known actress, Hedwig Niemann-Raabe, who wanted to play the lead role but who refused to play the final scene as written because "I would never leave [my] children." Ibsen accepted the difficult challenge of writing an alternative, "happy" ending himself rather than have someone else do it for him. In this version, Nora does not leave the house, but she is forced by Helmer to the doorway of the children's bedroom. Nora sinks by the door, and the curtain falls. It was this version that opened in Germany. Notably, Niemann-Raabe eventually reverted to the original text.

Ibsen's play has maintained its place in the popular repertoire and is regularly performed. Actresses such as Claire Bloom, Janet McTeer—who won a Tony Award (Antoinette Perry Award for Excellence in Theatre)—for the role, Cheryl Campbell, and Tara Fitzgerald have portrayed Nora onstage. This has fast become one of the most coveted female roles in drama. Helmer, the play's second lead, it is probably fair to say, has attracted fewer first-rank actors. One of the most unusual modern productions was a fascinating 2007 production by Lee Breur, which played at the Edinburgh Festival and which cast dwarves in the male roles in order to play with the gender bias in Nora's society. This version rendered comic Torvald's insistence on patronizing his "poor little Nora," especially since he was small enough to be (at one point, actually) picked up by his wife.

There have been three major film versions. Patrick Garland's film stars Claire Bloom as Nora, Anthony Hopkins as Torvald, and Ralph Richardson as Dr. Rank. Joseph Losey's stars Jane Fonda and rather awkwardly depicts some of the events that occur before the play. A low-budget version by David Thacker looks dreadful in some ways but nevertheless contains a series of fine performances, not least from Trevor Eve as Torvald.

Author of ClassicNote and Sources

Robert William, author of ClassicNote. Completed on June 18, 2008, copyright held by GradeSaver.

Updated and revised Adam Kissel August 02, 2008. Copyright held by GradeSaver.

Ibsen, Henrik (trans. Michael Meyer). A Doll's House (Ibsen Plays: Two). London: Methuen Drama, 2000.

Ibsen, Henrik. A Doll's House. No city: no publisher, 1879.

Ibsen, Henrik (trans. Charlotte Barslund and Frank McGuinness). A Doll's House. London: Faber and Faber, 1997.

Bradbrook, M.C. Ibsen the Norwegian: A Revaluation. London: Chatto and Windus, 1966.

Johnston, Brian. Ibsen's Selected Plays: A Norton Critical Edition. New York: W.W. Norton, 2004.

Meyer, Michael. Ibsen. Great Britain: Sutton Publishing, 1967.

Northam, John. Ibsen: A Critical Study. Cambridge: Cambridge University Press, 1973.

Shaw, George Bernard. The Quintessence of Ibsenism. London: Dover Publishing, 1891.

Steiner, George. The Death of Tragedy. London: Faber and Faber, 1961.

Essay: Influence of Antigone on A Doll's House

by Anonymous
October 14, 2001

It is very difficult to label something as a first in literature. Much the way inventions are often adaptations of previously patented objects, most authors borrow ideas and techniques form pre-existing media. In order to truly classify something as a first one must look for something entirely revolutionary, something that has never been done before. Two of these so called "firsts" include the first modern novel with Flaubert's **Madame Bovary** and what has been called the first modern play in Ibsen's **A Doll's House**. Regarding the latter, it is important to realize that while the play did break several molds which had endured for centuries, much was borrowed and adapted from past works. Of these, another "first" emerges for having shown a strong influence on Ibsen and his revolutionary play. Coincidentally, it is what historians refer to as on of the first plays in existence, Sophocles' Antigone.

In merely looking at the surface, one notices right away that both plays are significant in that they avoid the social temptation of using a man as a protagonist. Looking deeper into the stories, however, one can see that in even more contradiction with society, the female characters go against men. Both Antigone and Nora step into the spotlight as the female hero who has been put in a compromising situation and is forced to decide whether it is more important to follow what society dictates, or go with what they feel is moral and just.

Antigone is faced with the death of both brothers, one who is to be buried with full military rites, while the other, under dictate of the king, is to be cast aside and allowed to rot in the sun. She places family before the law, and ventures out to give her brother a proper burial. In A Doll's House, Nora too must decide where the line between right and wrong is drawn. In order to save her husband's life, Nora forges her father's name on a promissory note. Both women thus break the law using similar justifications. Antigone does so under the premise that the Gods dictated that all men deserved a proper burial. Likewise, Nora commits her crime with the belief that since it is saving a life, her situation is an exception to the rules.

The leading men in both works also have similar characterizations. Both Creon and Helmer are egotistical men, who put too much value on their position of authority; Creon so much so that he is willing to put a decree that defies the laws of the Gods. Furthermore, both are close-minded and too stubborn to see that they could be wrong. When Nora reveals her crime to Helmer, the audience expects to see a grateful and understanding husband, but instead is greeted with a spiteful and unappreciative man who does not see the true purpose of Nora's deed. Similarly, Creon, instead of seeing that his niece Antigone placed family and the Gods before the law of the land, solely sees that he has been disobeyed.

Both men worry about how their social status will be affected by the actions of the women; Creon is afraid he will look weak if he allows Antigone's deed to go unpunished, and Helmer is worried about allowing his wife to commit such a crime. One could argue that the true criminals are the men themselves, for not having the conscience to step down. Both men realize too late the consequences of their behavior. After yelling at Nora, and revealing to her in not so many words that she is merely a doll in his doll house, Helmer tries to apologize. Likewise, after much debate, Creon heads to the cave where he had exiled Antigone to free her. In both instances their apologies are too late. After Helmer's soliloquy, Nora walks out on her family to find a new life and discover herself. When Creon arrives to his destination, he finds Antigone hanged and his son dead by his own hand. It is due to both mens' stubbornness that their stories take this tragic turn.

While Sophocles and Ibsen are from two entirely different times and cultures, and although their writing styles differ dramatically, the influence of **Antigone** on the story of **A Doll's House** cannot be overlooked.

Essay: Burning Down the Doll House

by Noah David Safford
February 25, 2000

'Until death do us part.' Well, not always. Everywhere one looks, divorce is plaguing society, and it has become widely accepted throughout the world. Now the violent shredding of a family is shrugged off like the daily weather, and the treasured marriage vows have become nothing but a promise made to be broken. In the novel The Lost World, a divorce was described along with sports cars and money as success, not failure. The Norwegian play A Doll's House, by Henrik Ibsen, is a prime example of a relationship that didn't work. The marriage of Torvald and Nora Helmer had many problems, and was doomed because the husband and wife couldn't match up to the elements of a successful couple-hood. To keep a marriage alive and growing it must hold true to four qualities: love, communication, trust and loyalty, and perseverance. With the incorporation of these qualities any marriage would work.

Without love a relationship would probably not even begin. Two people meet, a friendship forms, and soon a romance blossoms. Though the basis for Nora and Torvald's relationship appeared to be centered around love, the needed balance was not obtained. Torvald didn't really love Nora; to him she was just another child to mind. He said, 'And I wouldn't want you to be any different from what you are-just my sweet little song bird. But now I come to think of it, you look rather-rather-how shall I put it? -rather as if you've been up to mischief today' (151). Calling his wife names such as 'skylark,' 'squirrel,' and 'spendthrift,' Torvald does not love his wife with the respect and sensitivity a man should. The main area where Torvald showed his lack of love for Nora was in the way he managed his house. Torvald was the owner of what he believed to be a perfect doll house. This doll house was first controlled by Nora's domineering father, and once Nora entered marriage, the titles and deeds to this doll house were handed over to Torvald. Torvald manipulated Nora, and then the children through her according to his wants, sure that he could never lose control over his precious doll house. This lack of love and imperious attitude would eventually ruin their marriage. Nora was the only one of the two partners who showed love for the other in this play. Going against all the odds a woman faced in the late nineteenth century, Nora went behind her husband's back, borrowed a large sum of money, forged her father's signature, and went on to pay it off with hopes of Torvald never hearing of it. She refused to be a doll, and would alternate personalities between 'Torvald's little skylark,' and 'Nora the intelligent and strong woman.' A balance of love between man and wife that is needed in any marriage was certainly not reached. This immoderate and unbalanced behavior definitely hurt the relationship of Torvald and Nora, but this was not the only factor that contributed to the break down of their partnership.

Two soul-mates need to communicate in a relationship. Before the wife pays the electric bills, she should inform her husband of the monetary situation. In the same sense, before the husband goes to the casino with his friends for beer and entertainment, he should tell his wife. The possibility exists that if Nora had informed Torvald of her plans to borrow money, a conflict such as this would have never happened. But that possibility is unrealistic. Torvald, a stubborn man in terms of money, could never accept the fact that even he, the powerful doll master, would need help from one of his unintelligent dolls. These two did not talk enough, as Nora says, 'We've been together for eight years now. Don't you realize that this is the first time that we two-you and I, man and wife-have had a serious talk together?' (225). The answer was no. The communication throughout their entire marriage was poor, as this quote illustrates. Throughout the entire play irony becomes a hammer that knocks the reader or viewer on the head, reminding him or her that the plot is ever thicker with each situation that arises. The truth is clear that when all of Nora's secret information is disclosed, something bad is bound to happen. Plainly, without a steady stream of communication a marriage can never hope to live onward.

Another problem with the communication was that neither spouse could truly trust the other. Without trust, marriage becomes impossible. Lacking honesty and loyalty, trust cannot be obtained. Two people cannot live together without trust for each other. If one spouse feels like he or she must constantly check up on the other, the marriage will fail. Torvald had almost no trust in Nora. In the first Act, he continually lampoons her for her flirtatious way of spending money, stating, 'It would be (sensible) if you really kept the money I give you, and actually bought something for yourself with it. But if it goes in with the housekeeping, and gets spent on all sorts of useless things, then I only have to pay out again' (150). If a man checks up on his wife like this any type of relationship is doomed from the start. Torvald's lack of trust toward Nora could be justified if she really were a spendthrift. In this case the wife would have to build up trust with her husband. As well as the husband would have to do the same in other circumstances. In order to gain this trust each individual must remain honest and loyal at all times. By being responsible in his or her own actions, trust can be earned through a husband and wife's honesty. With the amount of trust that Nora and Torvald have for each other, no marriage could be possible. But even united together these elements alone cannot completely hold a couple as one.

Life is a rough and tough road, and in order to navigate down its treacherous curves a pair must be able to persevere in difficult times. A couple can have a great bond, but in a time of pain or dilemma that bond can be forgotten and all their problems shadow the great relationship they have. If the two cannot pick up the pieces and move onward, only one fight or hard time can cause a couple to break up, . An attitude must be adopted in these times that simply says, 'I'm angry with you, but I will forgive you.' Hard events in life are inevitable, but not unbeatable. Torvald and Nora didn't have problems persevering because Torvald did all of the problem solving for them both, and took care of Nora's problems himself. Torvald did not act like this out of selfishness, but rather to be the dominate male in the relationship, not allowing Nora to think and act for herself. Because of Torvald's lack of love and trust, and abundance of control, Nora decided that to persevere would only result in more problems. Perseverance is only a good idea if the other three qualifications are met, because at that point only more problems will arise.

Nora and Torvald's marriage failed because they lacked in all of the qualifications for a successful marriage. And the marriage failed because of Torvald's imperious control over his family. If any type of doll house is present in a marriage such as that of the Helmers', it would be a serious impediment to any attempt at success. Before Nora leaves, she tells Torvald, 'I've been your doll-wife here, just as at home I was Papa's doll-child. And the children have been my dolls in their turn...That's what our marriage has been' (226). In order to ensure a wonderful and happy life together, any doll house must be burnt to the ground, and the lighter fluid must be the fuel bearing the names of love, trust, communication, and perseverance. When the smoke is cleared, the wonderful bond of marriage can be enjoyed to it's fullest extent, and until 'death do us part.'

Quiz 1

1. **For whom did the Nurse work for before taking care of Nora's children?**
   A. Nora's father and little Nora
   B. Dr. Skein and little Helmer
   C. Mrs. Linde and her children
   D. no one

2. **What is the sweet that Nora is forbidden to eat?**
   A. marzipan
   B. macaroons
   C. candy canes
   D. fruit cakes

3. **Dr. Rank is dying from what?**
   A. diseased liver
   B. fever of the brain
   C. dysentery
   D. consumption of the spine

4. **How are Nora and Mrs. Linde related?**
   A. as old enemies
   B. as childhood friends
   C. as mother and daughter
   D. as sisters

5. **Which of the following events is the subject of discussion at the very beginning of the play?**
   A. Krogstad and Christine's marriage
   B. Torvald's promotion to manager of the bank
   C. Torvald and Nora's trip to Italy
   D. Nora's deal with Krogstad

6. **Which of the following is not a part of Nora's dilemma stemming from her loan from Krogstad?**
   A. She forged a signature to obtain the loan
   B. She never told Torvald
   C. She is afraid her father will find out
   D. She can't convince Torvald not to fire Krogstad

7. **Torvald and Nora are preparing the house for what?**
   A. Easter
   B. Thanksgiving
   C. Nora's birthday
   D. Christmas

8. **Mrs. Linde and Torvald both call Nora**
   A. a robin
   B. a spendthrift
   C. a buttercup
   D. a lark

9. **When does Nora finally leave the sitting room?**
   A. Act II, Scene 1
   B. Act II, Scene 2
   C. Act III
   D. the end of Act I

10. **Nora flirts with Dr. Rank, showing him what?**
    A. her silk gloves
    B. her silk stockings
    C. her silk slip
    D. her new dress

11. **According to Torvald, it would be impossible to work with Krogstad because**
    A. Torvald becomes physically ill in Krogstad's presence
    B. Torvald is too jealous of Krogstad
    C. Nora would object
    D. Krogstad has physically threatened Torvald

12. **Which character says, "Bloody Hell!"?**
    A. Torvald
    B. Krogstad
    C. Nora
    D. Dr. Rank

13. **How does Dr. Rank inform Nora that he has reached the final stages of his illness?**
   A. he tells her while they are dancing
   B. he leaves a black cross on his visiting card
   C. he sends her a note
   D. he asks Torvald to tell her

14. **In the first act, why does Nora laugh aloud in front of Dr. Rank and Mrs. Linde?**
   A. Krogstad will be fired
   B. Mrs. Linde will be working for Torvald
   C. she will have so much more money
   D. so many people at the bank will be dependent on Torvald

15. **Which one of the following reasons does Mrs. Linde not give for coming to town?**
   A. to reconnect with Krogstad
   B. to find something to fill the emptiness of her life
   C. to seek employment
   D. to reenter society

16. **Which one of the following does Torvald not identify Nora with?**
   A. a child
   B. a puppy
   C. her father
   D. a squirrel

17. **What excuse does Nora give to explain why she did not have any ornaments?**
   A. she gave them to the less-fortunate
   B. the maid accidentally threw them away
   C. the cat tore them up
   D. the dog tore them up

18. **Krogstad has gotten a bad reputation because of a scandal in which he allegedly**
   A. blackmailed a coworker at the bank
   B. destroyed valuable bank documents
   C. stole money from the bank
   D. forged a signature

19. **Which character complains that society is being turned into a "sick house"?**
    A. Torvald
    B. Mrs. Linde
    C. Krogstad
    D. Dr. Rank

20. **Which one of these does Nora not explicitly question at the end of the play?**
    A. religion
    B. her father's love
    C. the love of her children
    D. her marriage

21. **Which of the following best symbolizes the character that Nora plays in her marriage with Torvald?**
    A. her cat
    B. the Tarantella
    C. the dress she wears to the party
    D. her new boots

22. **A Doll's House was considered a theatrical innovation because it altered the well-made play to include**
    A. a moral
    B. an unraveling
    C. a climax
    D. a discussion

23. **Mrs. Linde's character symbolizes all of the following except**
    A. the pitfalls of marrying for money
    B. Nora's potential future
    C. moral perfection
    D. the potential emptiness of motherhood

24. **The tarantella symbolizes all of the following except**
    A. Nora's role as performer for Torvald
    B. the equality of Nora and Torvald's marriage
    C. Nora's desire to retain Torvald's attention
    D. Nora's desire to rid herself of the poison that has developed out of her transaction with Krogstad

25. **Which of the following is used as a metaphor throughout the play?**

A. cutlery
B. glass figurines
C. light
D. music

Quiz 1 Answer Key

1. **(A)** Nora's father and little Nora
2. **(B)** macaroons
3. **(D)** consumption of the spine
4. **(B)** as childhood friends
5. **(B)** Torvald's promotion to manager of the bank
6. **(C)** She is afraid her father will find out
7. **(D)** Christmas
8. **(B)** a spendthrift
9. **(C)** Act III
10. **(B)** her silk stockings
11. **(A)** Torvald becomes physically ill in Krogstad's presence
12. **(C)** Nora
13. **(B)** he leaves a black cross on his visiting card
14. **(D)** so many people at the bank will be dependent on Torvald
15. **(D)** to reenter society
16. **(B)** a puppy
17. **(C)** the cat tore them up
18. **(D)** forged a signature
19. **(D)** Dr. Rank
20. **(C)** the love of her children
21. **(C)** the dress she wears to the party
22. **(D)** a discussion
23. **(C)** moral perfection
24. **(B)** the equality of Nora and Torvald's marriage
25. **(C)** light

Quiz 2

1. **When Nora leaves the sitting room to change into street clothes, this symbolizes**
   A. her hatred of Torvald
   B. her realization that she must take her children away from Torvald in order to raise them properly
   C. her desire to look like Mrs. Linde
   D. her break with her given role as mother and wife

2. **When Nora tries to leave the house in order to commit suicide while Torvald is reading Krogstad's letter, she throws on Torvald's domino, symbolizing**
   A. her desire to expose him to the world's scorn
   B. her desire to take Torvald's problems upon herself, sparing him the pain
   C. her desire to steal from him as he has stolen from her
   D. her dislike of the garment

3. **In the second act, Nora speaks to Dr. Rank about his impending death. While they speak, it grows dark, probably representing**
   A. Nora's choice to use her sexual power over Dr. Rank to ask him a favor and her subsequent moral blackening
   B. Nora's lust for Dr. Rank
   C. the affair that they are having behind Torvald's back
   D. Dr. Rank's desire to kill Nora

4. **The setting of the living room represents**
   A. that this is a situation specific to this particular family
   B. an attack on business
   C. that nothing really changes over the course of the play
   D. an attack on contemporary middle class values

5. **The play takes place around Christmas, a celebration of the birth of Jesus, most strongly symbolizing**
   A. Nora's ultimate decision to embrace Christianity
   B. the rebirth of the characters
   C. Mrs. Linde's spiritual guidance of Nora
   D. the Christian moral values of the play

6. **Which of the following characters does not experience some sort of awakening or rebirth during the course of the play?**
   A. Torvald
   B. Mrs. Linde
   C. Krogstad

D. Ivar

7. **Dr. Rank's illness represents**
   A. his penitence
   B. his moral corruption
   C. his wisdom
   D. his link to Mrs. Linde

8. **Which of the following characters does not subvert a traditional role?**
   A. Mrs. Linde
   B. Nora
   C. Ivar
   D. Dr. Rank

9. **The fact that Mrs. Linde usurps Krogstad's position at the bank symbolizes**
   A. a potential source of equality in their relationship
   B. her hatred of Krogstad
   C. Krogstad's desire to be dominated by a woman
   D. her belief in her superiority

10. **Torvald frequently calls Nora various small animals, signaling**
   A. her perception of herself as unfit for human existence
   B. his perception of her as a wild creature he has had to tame for the benefit of society
   C. her bizarre eating habits
   D. his perception of her as a toy or pet for his amusement

11. **"Come along, Mrs. Linde; the place will only be bearable for a mother now!" illustrates**
   A. Torvald's belief in a strict division of male and female spheres
   B. Nora's desire to painfully remind Mrs. Linde of the fact that Mrs. Linde is now childless
   C. Torvald's dislike of his children
   D. Dr. Rank's desire to painfully remind Mrs. Linde of the fact that she is now childless

12. **Nora's disbelief that her forgery, done out of love, could be considered illegal represents**
   A. her lack of understanding of the laws of her new country
   B. her lack of connection with and understanding of the real world
   C. her complete lack of morality despite Dr. Rank's counseling on the matter
   D. her pretending to be stupid in order to con Krogstad and Torvald out of more money

13. **"You are not your father's daughter for nothing." This quotation is part of the theme of**
    A. Mrs. Linde's amorous links to Nora's father
    B. Torvald's jealousy of Nora's father
    C. society's need to define women through men
    D. Nora's hatred of her mother

14. **For Torvald, Krogstad represents**
    A. his bad business sense
    B. his youthful impetuousness
    C. his wife's strongest passions
    D. the potential impurity of his own moral character

15. **When does the play break with the tradition of the well-made play?**
    A. when Nora questions Torvald's love of her
    B. when Nora tries to leave to commit suicide
    C. when Nora leaves at the very end
    D. when Nora tells Torvald to sit down because they need to talk

16. **The bond that Nora buys from Krogstad can also be seen as**
    A. a symbol of the bond between Krogstad and Torvald
    B. a symbol of the bond between Nora and Torvald
    C. a symbol of Nora's love for Italy
    D. a symbol of Nora's love for her dead father

17. **"I am afraid, Torvald, I do not exactly know what religion is." This quotation illustrates which theme?**
    A. Nora's need to question all established customs after her awakening
    B. Nora's unfamiliarity with the customs of her new country
    C. Nora's tendencies to lie
    D. Nora's stupidity

18. **Which of the following characters can be said to represent perfect morality?**
    A. Torvald
    B. Nora
    C. Dr. Rank
    D. None of the above

19. **What is the wonderful thing according to Nora?**

A. perfect equality in marriage

B. when all returns to what it was

C. Nora's death

D. the death of Torvald

20. **Whom does Nora first tell that a wonderful thing is going to happen?**

A. Torvald

B. Mrs. Linde

C. Krogstad

D. Dr. Rank

21. **Which quotation is an assumption at the heart of Nora's conception of the wonderful thing?**

A. "It gives me great pain, Torvald, for you have always been so kind to me, but I cannot help it. I do not love you any more."

B. "You know how devotedly, how inexpressibly Torvald loves me; he would never for a moment hesitate to give his life for me."

C. "Your squirrel would run about and do all of her tricks if you would be nice and do what she wants."

D. "Yes--you see, there are some people one loves best and others whom one would almost always rather have as companions."

22. **When does Nora tell Torvald that the idea of the wonderful thing first came to her?**

A. Act I

B. Act II

C. before the beginning of the play

D. Act III

23. **What prompts Nora to abandon her plan of suicide in favor of leaving her home and family?**

A. the fact that Torvald chooses to take the responsibility for the bond on himself in order to protect Nora and their marriage

B. the annoyance of having to leave the ball early at Torvald's insistence

C. the fact that Torvald does not choose to take the responsibility for the bond upon himself in order to protect Nora and their marriage

D. knowing that Dr. Rank will soon die

24. **Mrs. Linde is suspicious of Dr. Rank because of**

A. his inappropriately motivated interest in Mrs. Linde

B. his inappropriately motivated interest in Nora

C. his illness

D. his inappropriately motivated interest in Torvald

25. **Which relationship serves as the best foil for that of Nora and Torvald?**

A. Nora and Dr. Rank

B. Mrs. Linde and Krogstad

C. Nora and Krogstad

D. Mrs. Linde and Dr. Rank

Quiz 2 Answer Key

1. **(D)** her break with her given role as mother and wife
2. **(B)** her desire to take Torvald's problems upon herself, sparing him the pain
3. **(A)** Nora's choice to use her sexual power over Dr. Rank to ask him a favor and her subsequent moral blackening
4. **(D)** an attack on contemporary middle class values
5. **(B)** the rebirth of the characters
6. **(D)** Ivar
7. **(B)** his moral corruption
8. **(C)** Ivar
9. **(A)** a potential source of equality in their relationship
10. **(D)** his perception of her as a toy or pet for his amusement
11. **(A)** Torvald's belief in a strict division of male and female spheres
12. **(B)** her lack of connection with and understanding of the real world
13. **(C)** society's need to define women through men
14. **(D)** the potential impurity of his own moral character
15. **(D)** when Nora tells Torvald to sit down because they need to talk
16. **(B)** a symbol of the bond between Nora and Torvald
17. **(A)** Nora's need to question all established customs after her awakening
18. **(D)** None of the above
19. **(A)** perfect equality in marriage
20. **(B)** Mrs. Linde
21. **(B)** "You know how devotedly, how inexpressibly Torvald loves me; he would never for a moment hesitate to give his life for me."
22. **(C)** before the beginning of the play
23. **(C)** the fact that Torvald does not choose to take the responsibility for the bond upon himself in order to protect Nora and their marriage
24. **(B)** his inappropriately motivated interest in Nora
25. **(B)** Mrs. Linde and Krogstad

Quiz 3

1. **What instrument does Nora use to dance the tarantella?**
   A. trumpet
   B. triangle
   C. tuba
   D. tambourine

2. **Before the play, Nora obtained money in order to**
   A. buy Christmas decorations to replace the ones that were lost
   B. buy herself new clothes
   C. buy medicine to heal Torvald's illness
   D. take Torvald on holiday to recover from his illness

3. **An alternative ending to the play**
   A. written by William Shakespeare, showed a series of happy marriages following Nora's exit
   B. written by Ibsen, showed Nora's funeral one week after the end of Act Three
   C. written by Ibsen's mistress, showed Nora shooting Torvald at close range
   D. written by Ibsen, showed Nora revoking her decision to leave

4. **The children's names are**
   A. Nicole, Mitzi, and Hetzl
   B. Ivar, Bob, and Emmy
   C. Mitzl, Enza, and Heinrich
   D. Fritzi, Mitzi, and Joe

5. **August Strindberg felt that the play was**
   A. an outrageous defense of feminism
   B. missing the first scene
   C. better than any of his own
   D. a misogynist, fascist play

6. **In an 1898 speech, Ibsen described himself as**
   A. a feminist
   B. August Strindberg's biggest fan
   C. more of a poet and less of a social philosopher
   D. a philosopher rather than a poet

7. **One quotation from Ibsen reads, "A woman cannot be herself**
   A. unless married"
   B. during sex"
   C. in modern society"
   D. when married"

8. **Ibsen believed his play to advocate the necessity for**
   A. animal rights
   B. better knowledge of the tarantella
   C. self-liberation
   D. women's liberation

9. **Torvald's holiday is to**
   A. Sweden
   B. Norway
   C. a cold climate
   D. a warm climate

10. **The play is set in**
   A. one room
   B. two rooms
   C. four rooms
   D. three rooms

11. **Nora's forgery is**
   A. signing Dr. Rank's signature
   B. signing Krogstad's signature
   C. signing her father's signature
   D. signing her husband's signature

12. **Krogstad is an employee of**
   A. the local shop
   B. the bank
   C. the post office
   D. the hospital

13. **Who says, "One has to live, doctor"?**
   A. Helmer
   B. Mrs. Linde
   C. Nora
   D. Dr. Rank

14. **In the first act, Nora offers a macaroon to**
   A. Torvald
   B. the nurse
   C. the children
   D. Dr. Rank

15. **What does Nora say upon being told that the law "does not concern itself with motives"?**
   A. "Why not?"
   B. "My motives are the law"
   C. "Then the law must be very stupid"
   D. "I never thought otherwise"

16. **What sort of ball is being held?**
   A. buffet
   B. foam party
   C. dinner party and dancing
   D. fancy-dress

17. **Where is the ball being held?**
   A. at the Helmers'
   B. at the Stenborgs'
   C. in the village hall
   D. downstairs

18. **When is the ball being held?**
   A. Christmas Day
   B. Christmas Eve
   C. Easter Sunday
   D. Boxing Day

19. **At the end of Act One, Nora worries that**
   A. her children might catch Dr. Rank's illness
   B. her children might run away
   C. Krogstad might threaten her children
   D. her own moral corruption might poison her children

20. **At the start of Act Two, Nora is**
   A. taking up the carpets
   B. endlessly walking to and fro
   C. blowing out the candles
   D. throwing Christmas decorations at the wall

21. **At the start of Act Two, Nora seems to be considering**
   A. burning down her house
   B. playing the tambourine
   C. leaving the house
   D. learning the tarantella

22. **In what season is the play set?**
   A. Spring
   B. Winter
   C. Autumn
   D. Summer

23. **Dr. Rank is ill because**
   A. his father kept mistresses
   B. his father died
   C. he ate uncooked chicken
   D. his father beat him

24. **Nora is going to the party dressed as**
   A. a prostitute
   B. Marilyn Monroe
   C. a songbird
   D. a Neapolitan fisher-girl

25. **Who does Nora describe as Torvald's oldest friend?**

A. herself
B. Mrs. Linde
C. Krogstad
D. Dr. Rank

Quiz 3 Answer Key

1. **(D)** tambourine
2. **(D)** take Torvald on holiday to recover from his illness
3. **(D)** written by Ibsen, showed Nora revoking her decision to leave
4. **(B)** Ivar, Bob, and Emmy
5. **(A)** an outrageous defense of feminism
6. **(C)** more of a poet and less of a social philosopher
7. **(C)** in modern society"
8. **(C)** self-liberation
9. **(D)** a warm climate
10. **(A)** one room
11. **(C)** signing her father's signature
12. **(B)** the bank
13. **(B)** Mrs. Linde
14. **(D)** Dr. Rank
15. **(C)** "Then the law must be very stupid"
16. **(D)** fancy-dress
17. **(B)** at the Stenborgs'
18. **(D)** Boxing Day
19. **(D)** her own moral corruption might poison her children
20. **(B)** endlessly walking to and fro
21. **(C)** leaving the house
22. **(B)** Winter
23. **(A)** his father kept mistresses
24. **(D)** a Neapolitan fisher-girl
25. **(D)** Dr. Rank

Quiz 4

1. **Which character in the play is described as rich?**
   A. Torvald
   B. Mrs. Linde
   C. Krogstad
   D. Dr. Rank

2. **Mrs. Linde's husband**
   A. dies in Act Two
   B. visits the house in Act Three
   C. died before the play began
   D. visits the house in Act One

3. **Who else describes Nora in diminutive terms as a squirrel and a songbird, other than Helmer?**
   A. Mrs. Linde
   B. Nora herself
   C. Dr. Rank
   D. none of the above

4. **Nora's father, according to Helmer, was**
   A. not, in fact, her father
   B. "the best man I have ever had the pleasure of meeting"
   C. "not a man of unassailable reputation"
   D. abhorrent

5. **Helmer thinks Nora is worried about Krogstad**
   A. burning their house
   B. attacking them physically
   C. besmirching their name in the newspapers
   D. becoming ill

6. **Nora is actually worried about Krogstad**
   A. besmirching their name in the newspapers
   B. kidnapping one of their children, Emmy
   C. revealing her secret to Torvald
   D. becoming ill

7. **Nora does not rip up Krogstad's letter to Helmer because**
   A. she does not have the key to the letterbox
   B. she is too scared
   C. it is engraved on a stone tablet
   D. it is never written

8. **The sound heard at the end of the play is**
   A. the songbird singing
   B. Helmer weeping
   C. the front door closing
   D. a dog barking

9. **Dr. Rank speaks about his father's wild life and regrets that**
   A. his dog never met his father
   B. his father died
   C. he never confronted his father
   D. he never got the chance to experience such pleasures

10. **What color are Nora's silk stockings?**
   A. flesh-colored
   B. the green of a songbird's wing
   C. red
   D. green

11. **Nora tells Dr. Rank that he can**
   A. sleep with her
   B. learn from her how to dance the tarantella
   C. tell Helmer her secret
   D. imagine that she is dancing the tarantella for him

12. **Which character confesses their love for Nora?**
   A. Mrs. Linde
   B. The Nurse
   C. Krogstad
   D. Dr. Rank

13. **Which character regrets their life passing without having left a mark?**
   A. Torvald
   B. Mrs. Linde
   C. Nora
   D. Dr. Rank

14. **Ibsen's first name is**
   A. Henrik
   B. Heinrich
   C. Maxim
   D. Anton

15. **When Krogstad enters in Act Two,**
   A. he is jubilant, dancing and singing
   B. he has yet to be sacked
   C. he tries to attack Nora
   D. he has been sacked

16. **When Krogstad says, "Under the ice? Down in the cold, black water?" he is guessing that Nora is considering**
   A. suicide by drowning
   B. a sailing trip
   C. swimming
   D. trying to escape via submarine

17. **Who corrects Nora's dancing of the tarantella?**
   A. Torvald
   B. Mrs. Linde
   C. Krogstad
   D. Dr. Rank

18. **Who plays the piano as Nora practices the tarantella?**
   A. Helmer
   B. first Nora, then Helmer, and finally Dr. Rank
   C. Dr. Rank, and then Mrs. Linde
   D. Nora herself

19. **When Helmer corrects Nora's dancing of the tarantella, what becomes symbolically clear?**
    A. her desire to be somebody else
    B. Helmer's control over her
    C. the way she plays a part for Helmer
    D. all of the above

20. **"She just gets scared like a child sometimes." Who is describing Nora?**
    A. Helmer
    B. Mrs. Linde
    C. Krogstad
    D. Dr. Rank

21. **At the start of Act Three, the Helmers are**
    A. asleep
    B. outside
    C. sitting in the room in silence
    D. at the dance

22. **How is the Helmers' sitting room described?**
    A. exquisitely and richly furnished
    B. clearly a family room: the children's toys lie on the floor
    C. comfortably, tastefully, but not expensively furnished
    D. a mess, macaroons scattered across the floor

23. **Which character took care of a helpless mother and two little brothers?**
    A. Helmer
    B. Mrs. Linde
    C. Nora
    D. Dr. Rank

24. **Who prevents Krogstad from taking his letter back?**
    A. Torvald
    B. Mrs. Linde
    C. Nora
    D. Dr. Rank

25. **Nora's Italian costume includes**

A. a pizza

B. no shawl at all

C. a large red shawl

D. a large black shawl

Quiz 4 Answer Key

1. **(D)** Dr. Rank
2. **(C)** died before the play began
3. **(B)** Nora herself
4. **(C)** "not a man of unassailable reputation"
5. **(C)** besmirching their name in the newspapers
6. **(C)** revealing her secret to Torvald
7. **(A)** she does not have the key to the letterbox
8. **(C)** the front door closing
9. **(D)** he never got the chance to experience such pleasures
10. **(A)** flesh-colored
11. **(D)** imagine that she is dancing the tarantella for him
12. **(D)** Dr. Rank
13. **(D)** Dr. Rank
14. **(A)** Henrik
15. **(D)** he has been sacked
16. **(A)** suicide by drowning
17. **(A)** Torvald
18. **(B)** first Nora, then Helmer, and finally Dr. Rank
19. **(D)** all of the above
20. **(A)** Helmer
21. **(D)** at the dance
22. **(C)** comfortably, tastefully, but not expensively furnished
23. **(B)** Mrs. Linde
24. **(B)** Mrs. Linde
25. **(D)** a large black shawl

Printed in Great Britain
by Amazon

60613419R00050